Mirrors in Mark

Mirrors in Mark
(and in other New Testament writings)

EDMOND SMITH

RESOURCE *Publications* • Eugene, Oregon

MIRRORS IN MARK (AND IN OTHER NEW TESTAMENT WRITINGS)

Copyright © 2014 Edmond Smith. All rights reserved. Except for brief quotations in critical publications or reviews, no part of this book may be reproduced in any manner without prior written permission from the publisher. Write: Permissions. Wipf and Stock Publishers, 199 W. 8th Ave., Suite 3, Eugene, OR 97401.

Resource Publications
An Imprint of Wipf and Stock Publishers
199 W. 8th Ave., Suite 3
Eugene, OR 97401

www.wipfandstock.com

ISBN 13: 978-1-4982-0270-1

Manufactured in the U.S.A.   09/16/2014

All Bible quotations, unless otherwise quoted, are taken from the New International Version, The Zondervan Corporation, 1986.

To Kerryn, my lovely wife, who patiently typed up *Mirrors in Mark* with all the complexities connected with the manuscript.

To my family for their encouragement and support, and in particular to Belinda for extra help.

To Dawn who gave her time sacrificially to make *Mirrors in Mark* presentable for publication.

"I think (the divine words) are like a mirror, in which one can see oneself and the movements of one's own heart"

—Athanasius, Bishop of Alexandria, 296-373

Contents

Preface | ix
Introduction | xi

1. Mirrors in Mark (The beginning of the Gospel) | 1
2. Mirrors in Romans (Salvation for Jew and Gentile) | 32
3. Mirrors in Galatians (Righteousness by faith in Christ) | 45
4. Mirrors in Ephesians (God's plan for the church) | 53
5. Mirrors in Philippians (Joy in the Lord) | 64
6. Mirrors in 1 Timothy (Instruction for governing the church) | 71
7. Mirrors in Titus (What constitutes doing good) | 83
8. Mirrors in Philemon (A runaway slave now "useful") | 85
9. Mirrors in Hebrews (Jesus, our great high priest) | 87
10. Mirrors in James (The royal law) | 96
11. Mirrors in 1 Peter (Service and suffering in hope) | 105
12. Mirrors in 2 Peter (Always remember) | 115
13. Mirrors in Jude (On contending for the faith) | 125
14. Mirrors in Revelation ("Come, Lord Jesus") | 135

Preface

MANY EFFORTS HAVE BEEN made to discover literary structures in the Bible, particularly in the Old Testament. It is common knowledge that Jesus' words and works were first recalled in oral traditions before they were finally written down with apostolic authority. It makes sense that mnemonic devices, common to ancient peoples, were employed to impress the mind with the treasured memories of Jesus' revelation.

It may have appeared I sailed solo to discover with excitement the remarkable patterns of the New Testament books enclosed in this volume, but acknowledgment is due for the various scholars who had explored already the books of the New Testament here omitted. They have searched out quite successfully such books as John, 1 Corinthians and 1 John. They provided inspiration to help me in searching out the other Scriptures listed, and there are further "islands" in the "archipelago" of God's word that in varying degrees are yet to be explored (certainly on my part), hence the omission here of such large books as Matthew and Luke, 2 Corinthians, 1 and 2 Thessalonians.

Two authors in particular through their skill and navigation have provided affirmation for the approach adopted in *Mirrors in Mark*. They are: Kenneth Bailey the author of *Poet and Peasant* and *Through Peasant Eyes*, and David Dorsey the author of *The Literary Structure of the Old Testament*.

Introduction

HOW DOES ANYONE REMEMBER their PIN number for banking purposes, or the passwords for their computers at work? For security reasons many have to change their passwords every month at work. Then, upon returning after a holiday break, some employees have not been able to get into their work computer because they have forgotten the elusive password. We may resort to memory tricks so as not to forget those simple numbers or words for "open sesame."

So much for what we ourselves muster to remember for personal advantage, but what happens when others seek in the public arena to teach or instruct us in a way that will make it memorable? Schoolteachers, preachers, conference leaders, university lecturers—all if they are worth their salt—will seek to make stick what they teach or preach or lecture or write by easy-to-remember devices. Some learners can be so "clever" that they remember much through alliteration and other devices without properly understanding the subject. In my high school days I passed my final year in Economics without understanding it—simply through memorizing the salient points and the correct answers with the aid of the mnemonic devices supplied by the teacher!

Apart from information required for examinations, conferences and such like, there is any amount of information that requires much retention, much that is to be obtained through books. Of course, it may be argued books are aplenty in our day and to a considerable degree we need not recall consciously what we have read or heard. Yet, the written and oral word, if it is worth retaining, is often made the more impressive if mnemonic devices are used to make the information stick.

Introduction

The New Testament is a collection of teaching stories (the Gospels and Acts), letters and written sermons (by Paul and others), and a vision (the book of Revelation).

With regard to the Gospels, it is commonly held that the four of them came to be written only after much of the material for them was circulating in oral form. After Jesus had ascended into heaven, what he taught and what he did was propagated and preserved at first *orally*. As Godet observed: "Certain cycles of narratives, more or less fixed, must have at that time formed themselves, consisting of a series of facts which (the apostles) loved to relate in one course of instruction".[1] As history has it when it is frequently repeated—the accounts of Jesus' teaching and deeds being history—the gospel story or history acquired a fixed and stereotyped form, while at the same time it assumed some variation arising from the individuality of those telling what happened, and some diversity arising from personal memories. The resort to mnemonic aids would make such a precious history stick in the minds of both narrator and listener.

Even when the gospels came to be written, the mnemonic devices were kept intact, as the written word was also meant to be impressionable.

Then, when the various letters of the New Testament came into existence, the attempt to create a lasting impression was the same. Mnemonic devices, according to the custom of the Greco-Roman age, and as they had been accordingly to the custom of the Jewish world, were employed to make the written work stick.

Some works in the New Testament appear to be not letters so much as written sermons (such as Hebrews and James). Even if this is true, efforts to make such works memorable sprang out of the usage of various devices.

As for the vision of Revelation, by its apocalyptic and dreamscape nature, the surreal images stick. Still, a certain structure—as I later on reveal—makes the whole vision more memorable.

The New Testament abounds in variegated ways by which its contents become more vivid. Of course, it is the Holy Spirit who brings its words to life most of all, but on a human and literary level there is nothing prosaic in the New Testament, for it brings about pleasure through word plays, assonances, alliteration, onomatopoeia (the formation of words from association of sound), repetition, parallelisms of thought, poetry, proverbs, parables, the speeding up and the slowing down of narrative for the sake of emphasis, and so on.

1. Godet, *Studies in the New Testament* 63.

Introduction

CHIASMI AND CATCHWORDS

MIRRORS OF MARK IS an attempt to highlight the use of chiasmi through catchwords and catchphrases in many of the New Testament books. This work is to aid the serious student of Scripture in understanding more deeply the contents of the divinely-inspired writings, assisting in making most vivid what is read, thus creating a more abiding impression in order to provoke one to live out the word.

Chiasmi are simply the inversion of themes, often including the use of catchwords or catchphrases to make the inversion obvious.

A simple inversion from Scripture is as follows:

A	B
The Sabbath was made	for man,
B	A
not man	for the Sabbath (Mark 2:27)

If lines were drawn to connect the A's and B's, they would form an X, which is the Greek letter Chi, hence the terms *chiasmus* (singular), *chiasmi* (plural).

Simple chiasmi abound in the New Testament within sentences, but chiasmi can be detected on a grander scale in the fairly long sections of prose. In fact, they may be found to cover entire books and going beyond the simple example above of A-B-B-A, employing continuously either catchwords or catchphrases to make the parallelisms obvious. In other words, in entire books there may be found catchwords and catchphrases that *mirror* one another from one block of subject to another, hence the title of this book – *Mirrors in Mark (and other New Testament writings)*.

As well as having been a long-established form of structure in ancient Israel orally and literally,[2] orally and literally it was commonly practiced elsewhere too. It still is used albeit subconsciously even in our day. Kenneth Bailey makes use of an amusing example of an oral use of it.[3] Here it is dialogue between two young men:

---

2. See David Dorsey's *The Literary Structure of the Old Testament*.
3. Bailey, *Poet and Peasant* 50.

Introduction

    A. Are you going to the party?"

        B. Can I bring a friend?"

            C. Boy or girl?"

                D. "What difference does it make?"

                D. "It is a matter of balance."

            C. "Girl."

        B. "OK."

    A. "I'll be there."

    Bailey goes on to say that in biblical literature the inversion principle is deliberate. He believes it is evident that it is deliberate, for often the heart of the parallelism is the climax, though in the conversation between the two young men, what transpires as 'D' (the heart of the chiasmi) is somewhat secondary for both speakers, and it may not always form the center of some extended chiasmi in the New Testament and be the core of it.

    It is not the aim of *Mirrors in Mark* to be drawn into analyzing closely small portions of any New Testament writing and causing the reader to lose out on seeing beauty in simplicity, and simplicity in beauty, among the inspired writings. I mean, can seeking chiasmi go too far? Bailey in *Poet and Peasant*, (67—68) finds in just Acts 2:23—26 a chiasmus that passes through stages A to J, and then in reverse J to A! Actually, Bailey's discovery is prima facie convincing. Yet, it is like looking into what appears as a beautiful face of a woman only to find by a long, long look that her face has some flaws and we lose sight of her overall beauty. *Mirrors in Mark* aims for beauty of a simple kind, of a kind that is not too analytical, that suggests by its simplicity something which makes the Scripture more memorable and a great pleasure to read. It is not that Scripture itself has flaws upon closer scrutiny, but that 'over-searching' for chiastic structures so often can distract from the broad picture. Admittedly, Bailey concedes that discovering chiastic structure just in two stanzas (two verses) is rare, as in the case of Acts 2:23—26, but surely there is not that much profit in searching for such a subtle but bewildering structure.

    Yet chiasmi can be on a large scale and still be of much profit.

    If it can be demonstrated first of all that the gospel of Mark has a recurring chiastic structure of A-B-B-A running through the whole gospel,

Introduction

then it is safe to say chiastic structure (though it may vary from one book to another) can be expected here and there throughout the rest of the New Testament, in accordance with what was a common device used by Jewish and other people of the ancient world.

Although paragraphing was not an original part of the New Testament writings, to the modern reader it is apparent that a work such as Mark's gospel can be divided into units and often paragraphs, hence the usually sound divisions in paragraphical form we have in modern versions of the New Testament. If it can be demonstrated that in Mark certain catchwords or catchphrases can "go missing" in one unit (likely in a paragraph in our version) and then reappear and are mirrored in a second one in close proximity, with two other units mirroring or bearing similarity in between, so completing one block of that gospel, the whole thing may simply be regarded as coincidence. Yet, if the same kind of pattern occurs in a second block . . . coincidental? Perhaps. What if one finds 19 blocks in Mark of the same ilk? Surely, it is more than a coincidence, and explains to a considerable degree how Mark's gospel had been written.

If Mark's gospel carries a recurring chiastic structure of A-B-B-A, it is reasonable to expect that other New Testament writings—if not all—resort to chiasmi, even though the pattern may differ from one book to another.

The essential aim of any oral or written word is that the message sticks. Chiasmi in the New Testament greatly help the gospel message, and with all its ramifications are graphic. May the following efforts help the reader gain further light on the nature of the divinely-inspired New Testament writings and magnify him who is the center of them all.

In the outlining of chiasmi throughout the following work, the words that appear in italics:

1. either underline the inverted words that are only mirrored within any one of many chiasmi in one book (as found typically in Mark's gospel)
2. are indicators within *one* large chiasmus that comprise a whole book in order to point forwards or backwards to mirroring catchwords or catchphrases (such as found with Romans).

1
Mirrors in Mark

VARIOUS ATTEMPTS HAVE BEEN made to discover chiasmi in Mark, but here we will set forth a simple outline of Mark as based on the pattern A-B-B-A recurring 19 times.

Scott[1] saw a rather intricate chiastic structure or parallel inversion in Mark—A-B-C-D-E-F-G-H-I-J, then back up the ladder to A again. He claimed the 'J' point that connected with Jesus' prophecy of his betrayal and passion and resurrection was in close proximity to the Transfiguration, and made it appear to be the heart of Mark. Scott was influenced in this through his discovery (based on the Greek text with no variants) that the gospel contained 11,050 words all told, if any of the suspect endings beyond 16:8 are not included. Before the episode to do with Jesus' prophecy of his death there are 5,393 words; after it, there are 5,447 words. The passage was slightly off center, but for Scott it meant the Transfiguration lay at the heart of Mark's gospel, taking into account other considerations, which we will not pursue.

Scott's arrangement of inverted parallelism in Mark, however, is unconvincing. Mark 5, 7 and 13 as whole chapters go missing from the parallelisms. And did Mark so contrive his words that he counted them out one by one for the sake of making the Transfiguration the core of the Gospel? Most importantly, not much heed was paid to catchwords or catchphrases in Scott's research.

---

1. Scott, *Chiastic Structure: A Key to the Interpretation of Mark's Gospel*, "Biblical Theological Bulletin," No. 15, January 1985

Mirrors in Mark (and in other New Testament Writings)

Another scholar, Breck,[2] believed he saw 70 chiasmi in Mark, together with "some (non-Markan) traditional verses." To Breck's credit, most of his inverted parallelisms are simple enough for mnemonic purposes, but the sheer weight of so many militates against the original purpose of ancient parallelisms, though the counterclaim may be that the ancient powers of recollection could absorb 70 chiasmi. Unfortunately, Breck held that various parts are un-Markan or pre-Markan, and are to be discounted and dismissed when chiastic structure is to be considered.

Dart[3] may have useful advice about chiastic structure, but his beliefs about the origin of Mark make it difficult for those of evangelical persuasion to accept his chiastic structure of the gospel. Tradition makes no reference to any tampering with the gospel; tradition held that Mark wrote the gospel in its entirety as inspired by the memoirs of the apostle Peter; and that it had definite apostolic primogeniture.

Lund[4] warned against "subjective terms of thought and theme," otherwise chiasmi may degenerate into a voter's choice. He claimed chiasmi must be self-evident. Let the reader be the judge as to whether or not the following effort has been successful according to Lund's criterion.

Mark

Jesus Saving Servant of God

1.A Jesus Christ, the Son of God (Mark 1:1)

1.B The desert and the Spirit (Mark 1:2 –13)

1.C The publishing of Good News and following Jesus (Mark 1:14–28)

1.D At the door and lonely places (Mark 1:29-2:12)

1.E The Lake, Levi, and the Sabbath (Mark 2:13–3:19)

1.F The family and no league with Satan (Mark 3:20–35)

1.G The teacher and the lake, and seed (Mark 4:1–4)

1.H The home folk and twelve years (Mark 5: 1–6:6)

1.I Recognition and the loaves (Mark 6:6b–56)

1.J Unclean people and foreign soil (Mark 7:1-8:21)

---

2. Breck, *The Shape of Biblical Language* (1954)
3. Dart, *Decoding Mark* (2003)
4. Lund, *Chiasmus in the New Testament* (1942)

1.K Half-seeing and suffering (Mark 8:22–9:10)

1.L Jesus the Christ and arguments (Mark 9:11–41)

1.M Entering the kingdom and acceptance at home (Mark 9:42–10:34)

1.N Going ahead and following, and the two requests (Mark 10:32–11:11)

1.O Attempting to arrest Jesus, the question of belief (Mark 11:12–12:12)

1.P Lordship, error and right (Mark 12:13–40)

1.Q Women giving much, knowing and not knowing the Day (Mark 12:41–14:9)

1.R The betrayal and the two cups (Mark 14:10–52)

1.S Ill-treatment, denial and confession (14:53–15:20)

1.T Building the temple in three days, the centurion (15:21–16:8)

The longer ending of Mark (16:9–20)

1.A JESUS CHRIST, THE SON OF GOD (MARK 1:1)

Mark's gospel has a simple introduction. His purpose in writing his gospel can stand apart from the recurring chiasmi A-B-B-A, upon which the rest of the gospel stands.

While there is doubt surrounding the authenticity of the wording "the son of God" because some early manuscripts did not have it, nevertheless important manuscripts did. Was the wording omitted earlier on because the second gospel seems to say little about Jesus being the son of God, focusing instead on him as the servant of God? In the light of Mark 12:35f and 15:39, there is every good reason to believe the words "the son of God" should be retained. The irony for Mark is that even though Jesus was the Christ (King) and the son of God, he was the true and humble servant who proved by such service to be none other than what was declared by Mark right at the beginning of his gospel.

1.B THE DESERT AND THE SPIRIT (MARK 1:2 -13)

The first chiasmus is encountered here in the words that follow the brief introduction of 1:1.

For Mark the good news about Jesus began with the ministry of John the Baptist in the desert (vv.2,3). John is viewed as a messenger, a forerunner for the Messiah. In Malachi it was predicted there would be a messenger before the Messenger, who would be the Lord or "the Messenger of the covenant" (Mk 14:24). John appears in the desert, signifying mankind is desert-like in their ways, like withering grass and fading flowers, in contrast to the word of God (Isa 40:30–8).

John came to baptize those of Israel who repented of their ways for the forgiveness of sins and in preparation for the baptism of the Holy Spirit. Repentance and forgiveness of sin is one thing, but to be empowered by the Holy Spirit in order to be holy in one's ways from then on was supreme, and fittingly enough it requires Christ alone to baptize men for the actual filling of the Spirit.

In a sense, what are to be the two catchwords in *desert* and *messenger* "go missing" when the gospel narrative is taken up with the next subject of John baptizing all those who desired to repent upon hearing him. The promising catchwords of *desert* and *messenger* together "go missing," being replaced by the potential catchwords *baptize* and the *Spirit* in the next paragraph, the two that immediately appear again in the unit following that one. So *baptize* and the *Spirit* are the catch-words for the two middle units or paragraphs, the last unit being the one where we see *desert* and *messenger* reappearing (1:1).

The desert and the Spirit

    A. John sent into *the desert* as *the messenger* (1:2–3)

        B. John *baptizing* in preparation for the baptism of *the Spirit* by Jesus (1:4–8)

        B. John *baptizing* Jesus who has *the Spirit* descend on him (1:9–11)

    A. Jesus sent into *the desert* where *angels* minister to him (1:12–13)

The core of the above chiasmus has *baptize* and *the Spirit* mirroring one another. The mirroring, while it in no way discounts the momentous appearance of John the Baptist in the desert to baptize those who would repent for the forgiveness of their sins, compels us to see both the comparison and a certain contrast between John's baptism of others and that of his baptism of Jesus. Many came to be baptized upon confession of their sins, but with the baptism of Jesus by John the evidence of Jesus' son-ship is manifest. Mark is silent about John asking Jesus why he should be baptized—instead, he shows his baptism was to disclose his son-ship, qualified to baptize others with the Spirit.

Mirroring the narrative concerning the sending of John to the desert as the messenger for Jesus (1:2-3) is the narrative about the Spirit sending Jesus to the desert (1:12-13). For Mark it is back to the desert—not for us as readers to witness people repenting for forgiveness but to see Jesus in the power of the Spirit resisting Satan and being rewarded with the angels serving him. In the original language "angel" and "messenger" are the same word. John was Jesus' messenger, the angels (messengers) prove to be so for the Father, doubtlessly relaying the Father's word of endorsement, the Son being praised for resisting the Adversary. Jesus' trust in the Father was also evident when surrounded by wild animals in addition to facing Satan. Nothing is explicitly said of the wild animals ever threatening Jesus but Jesus doubtlessly was facing natural and supernatural aggression to endorse what the Father had said about his son at his baptism.

All these and other things can be teased out of Mark's words when we observe the mirroring that goes on in the narrative.

1.C THE PUBLISHING OF GOOD NEWS AND FOLLOWING JESUS (MARK 1:14-28)

The second chiasmus immediately follows the first. The A-B-B-A parallelism is in Mark 1:14-28 too, as we note the pattern: the publishing of the good news (vv.14-15); the matter about following Jesus (vv.16-18); following Jesus again considered (vv.19-20); then again the publishing of good news (vv.21-28).

After John was imprisoned, Jesus is said to have gone into Galilee to publish the good news of God, which is synonymous with what Mark stated at the beginning ("the good news of Jesus Christ, the Son of God"). We are to understand that the Kingdom of God was "near" in the sense that in the person of Jesus the Kingdom came near to Jesus' hearers.

It was necessary in the light of the good news being published that Jesus would soon call on others to spread his teaching. Yet initially, Jesus alone is found exercising a teaching ministry that is accompanied by miracles to show he himself is the Messiah. Teaching accompanied by an

Mirrors in Mark (and in other New Testament Writings)

exorcism focuses on Jesus' messianic power, with the chosen followers in those early stages viewed as onlookers.

The publishing of Good News and following Jesus

    A. Jesus in *Galilee* preaching good news (1:14-15)

        B. Jesus says to Andrew and Peter "Come, *follow* me" and they *left* their nets to do so (1:16-18).

        B. James and John also *follow* Jesus, *leaving behind* their father and the hired servants (1:19-20).

    A. Jesus in Capernaum exorcises an unclean spirit from a man in the synagogue so that the onlookers exclaim "What is this? A new teaching—and with authority!" The word about Jesus spreads quickly over all *Galilee* (1:21-28).

One catchword ("Galilee") is found linking 1:14-15 with 1:21-28 but, while "Galilee" may beg to be distinguishable as a catchword, it is plain that the good news embodied brand-new teaching and took on flesh in revealing Jesus' power over evil spirits, thus revealing the nearness of the Kingdom in Jesus, and thus put Galilee "on the map" throughout the land.

With respect to the calling of the four fishermen, a number of similarities between the two episodes are quite obvious. One difference bears pondering: Andrew and Peter were casting their nets, while the other two brothers were repairing theirs. Jesus either may call when one is actually in the act of carrying out a vocation or in preparing to pursue it. One act may be no easier to do for Jesus' sake than the other, but the emphasis in both cases, according to the original, is not on what was given up but in following Jesus.

1.D AT THE DOOR AND LONELY PLACES (MARK 1:29-2:12)

Mark and Luke place the leaving of Capernaum's synagogue on Jesus' part with the entry of Jesus into the house of Simon, whose mother-in-law was sick with a fever. Mark and Luke, more than Matthew, see that day in the synagogue at Capernaum, then in Simon's house followed by the curing of

Simon's mother-in-law and the milling crowds after sunset in seeking healing, as "A Busy Day"(to borrow one scholar's vivid description).

Yet, Mark "bends" the gospel story in his unique style to set up another A-B-B-A structure to follow the first two, shifting the account of the early cleansing of a leper to complete the chiasmus.

At the door and lonely places

A. Jesus leaves the synagogue at *Capernaum* and heals Simon's mother-in-law before sunset, when the whole town gathers *at the door* and Jesus heals many (1:29–34).

> B. Next morning when it is barely daylight, Jesus goes to a *lonely place* to pray before he goes preaching in large *villages or towns* near cities.

> B. A cleansed leper disobeys Jesus' strong warning not to tell anyone of the healing and Jesus is compelled to stay outside any *town or walled place* and retreat to *lonely places* (1:40–45).

A. Jesus is found in *Capernaum* once again, with so many people coming together that there was not even room left *at the door* where Jesus was (2:1–12).

Of course, catchwords such as *the door* and *lonely place(s)* would have little meaning without knowing the narrative of Mark but, in knowing the narrative, they serve as hooks on which to hang the tapestry of the narrative—the sequence of events with the beauties of comparison and contrast.

What is all disclosed in Mark 1:29-34 is part of "A Busy Day," a day that doubtless left Jesus tired and caused him to desire a solitary place to pray very early next morning.

When Simon and his friends discover him in the solitary place, Jesus says that he must defy the wishes of many and not linger at Capernaum, since he had come to earth to preach and heal in other places as well.

When Simon catches up with Jesus, villages (places around towns or cities) are spoken about. Then, when the leper shoots his mouth off indiscreetly, it is said Jesus could no longer enter a town. In the first case smaller groups of houses near towns in the country are in mind; while in the second case large walled places or towns are in mind. It may not mean larger places such as cities were avoided from the start, but only that there was more of a concentration of preaching in smaller places, where the wrong kind of publicity would not run riot. At this point in Mark's gospel we meet for the first time what has been dubbed "The Messianic Secret." It has baffled many—Jesus did much to have the excitement die down. As well as misguided people being caught up with the miracles and not the message of the gospel, there was the fear that many in larger places would only see a Messiah in Jesus of their own making. The good news was more than the performance of miracles—people were expected to repent and believe the nearness of the Kingdom arose in Jesus, who expected Israel to seek forgiveness of sins in him.

Indeed, it is apposite that Mark allows the event of the healing of the paralytic to follow on from that which has been known as "The Messianic Secret" for, while Jesus had sought lonely places, there would be no secret as to his authority to forgive sin (2:1–12).

Here lies the balance: once at a door Jesus healed many of various diseases and demon-possession, but once at a door he not only healed but astonishingly forgave a man of his sins too.

1.E THE LAKE, LEVI, AND THE SABBATH (MARK 2:13-3:19)

Next we find two incidents that have to do with the Lake of Galilee and Levi. These two incidents flank two that are linked with each other since they deal with the issue of Jesus' view of the Sabbath.

The Lake, Levi, and the Sabbath

- A. Jesus adopts another disciple by *the lake*, when he encounters *Levi* (2:13–2:22)

  - B. One *Sabbath* the Pharisees question Jesus about doing what is *unlawful* to do on the Sabbath (2:22–28).

  - B. On another *Sabbath* it is Jesus in turn found asking what is *unlawful* (3:1–6)

- A. Jesus is down by the *lake*, presumably withdrawing from the plotting of the Pharisees and the Herodians, before he goes up a mountain where he chooses 12 apostles, among whom is *Levi* (3:7–18).

While the link between two Sabbath incidents is quite obvious, irrespective of time they have been matched—note the working "another time" in Mark 3:1—thus the link between the two pieces of narrative to do with the Lake and the Levi may appear a little tenuous as far as closeness of time is concerned. Still, they will be seen as well-crafted for linkage when it is realized that as Jesus progresses in his ministry he meets growing opposition. The sore need to groom men, who include Levi, to become apostles becomes apparent. So, besides the two flanking pieces of narrative having in common a reference to a large crowd gathering around Jesus when he is beside the lake, Levi comes into the picture each time—first as a new follower of Jesus with his hosting of a dinner that defines quite sharply Jesus' mission to save sinners and not the self-righteous, then second as more than a follower when he is chosen to be one of twelve apostles. While Levi was only one of twelve to be chosen for apostleship, apostleship was a rare privilege, and perhaps he took on a new name for even a higher calling than a follower when numbered among the twelve—that of "Matthew" ("gift of God.")

1.F THE FAMILY AND NO LEAGUE WITH SATAN (MARK 3:20–35)

Mark does not follow Matthew and Luke by telling why the accusation levelled at Jesus of healing people through the power of Beelzebub arose. It arose with the healing of a dumb demoniac. Instead, it was Mark's desire to align the opinion of Jesus' family with that of the scribes and the Pharisees—Jesus' family claiming their acclaimed relative was "out of his mind," and the scribes and Pharisees insisting he was in league with the prince of demons whenever he healed.

The alignment of opinion meant both Jesus' family and his opponents in the scribes and the Pharisees sought to hinder his ministry. More or less, Mark is putting the family in the same company as those who said Jesus was demon-possessed. To Jesus' family it seemed he was unbalanced in busyness, while the others branded him as unbalanced in healing with the aid of Beelzebub. Either way he was unbalanced, though the harsher words by Jesus in answer to any perverted view of him would be directed to the teachers of the law who had come all the way from Jerusalem.

It is almost as if the teachers of the law were making capital out of what Jesus' family said of him, but it is not necessary to draw such a conclusion that Mark does not appear to make. Mark is only saying there was an alignment of opinion to a degree.

Mirrors in Mark (and in other New Testament Writings)

The family and no league with Satan

- A. Those *belonging to him* (translations consistently use this expression to mean Jesus' family) sought to lay hold of Jesus since they reckoned he had lost his mind (3:20-21)
  - B. If Jesus was exorcizing in league with Satan, then Satan's house could not stand but had to be divided. It was claimed Jesus literally *has Beelzebub* (2:22-26)
  - B. To the contrary, Jesus was robbing the strong man's house. Jesus warned his opponents about blaspheming against the Holy Spirit, as they claimed he *"has an evil spirit"* (2:27-30).
- A. Jesus' *mother and brothers* (those who belonged to him) attempted to call him out of the crowd but he told those sitting around him that they were his true mother and brothers and sisters (2:31-35).

As for 3:22-30, the case is first stated negatively Satan cannot stand, his house cannot if he is divided against himself. Still, the negative case has its positive: "his end has come." When the case is stated positively (vv.27-30), Satan is portrayed as a strong man who has been tied up and robbed. There is solemn warning against believing Jesus had an evil spirit, he clearly was doing what he did by the Holy Spirit. Then Mark returns to the question of Jesus' family to complete this panel of his gospel (vv.34-35).

Like Mark, Matthew defines Jesus' true family after the two parables concerning Satan, but Mark's shorter account of the two parables, together with their application, shows him speeding up the account in order to draw a closer link between Jesus being regarded by his family as losing his mind and him defining who his closest family is.

1.G THE TEACHER AND THE LAKE, AND SEED (MARK 4:1-41)

As the record in Mark has it, little has been said about what Jesus actually taught. Up to this point, little if anything has been said about what it means to be in the Kingdom, about those who hear but do not hear what Jesus is saying, about the nature of the Kingdom, of the way the Kingdom will eventuate.

1 Mirrors in Mark

In this panel Jesus is portrayed as the Teacher by the lake explaining the mystery of the kingdom, and then as Teacher on the lake itself when a storm threatens.

The teacher and the lake, and seed

A. Jesus by *the lake* begins to *teach*. He relates a parable of considerable length. The Kingdom is not directly referred to in the parable itself, for the parable of the Sower and the Seed fixes itself entirely on the various reactions Jesus' hearers have on hearing the word of God. Hearing aright is emphasized (4:1–25).

B. Then a parable is related to the nature of the *Kingdom of God*—what *the Kingdom of God is like*. The *growth of grain seed* illustrates it (4:26–29).

B. Another parable explains what *the Kingdom of God is like*. It also refers to *growth of seed*—this time mustard seed (4:30–34).

A. At evening Jesus suggests he and his disciples cross *the lake*. On the lake a storm springs up and the disciples awake their sleeping Teacher with the cry, "*Teacher*, don't you care if we die?"

While Matthew and Luke obviously mean for us to view Jesus as teaching by the Lake of Galilee, it is Mark who alone employs the word "teach" to show Jesus was explaining how to hear what he was saying, afterwards pointing out emphatically (as Mark has it) to disciples that what they heard from him was designed to be disclosed, that they must pay close attention to his teaching as more fruit is promised if it is heeded. Some say the lamp of which Mark speaks refers to witnessing as light-bearers, but I believe Bock is correct when he says: "It is his message that is light."[5] Bearing witness is crucial but at this point Jesus is concerned that his fledging disciples listen carefully to what he says, as light through his teaching was revealing the previously undisclosed mysteries of the Kingdom to them.

Mark groups two parables for their similarity as touching on the nature of the Kingdom. The parable of The Seed Growing Secretly (vv. 26–29) is unique to Mark. This parable teaches we are limited to sowing. God does

---

5. Bock, *The NIV Application Bible – Luke*, 233

the rest. He will bring in the Kingdom eventually (not immediately as many had hoped in Jesus' time).

Unique also to Mark is the form of address Jesus' disciples adopted when crying out for Jesus to save them in the storm on the lake. Matthew tells us Jesus was called on as "Lord," Luke "Master." Mark refers to the title "Teacher" to draw attention to the fact that when Jesus told his own to listen with care to what he had to say back on the shore of the lake earlier in the day, Jesus' intention was for them to see him as their Teacher who would listen with care to their desperate cry for help and save them. His intention was to spare their lives. He was not to groom them to be apostles in vain.

1.H THE HOME FOLK AND TWELVE YEARS (MARK 5: 1-6:6)

Once Jesus and his disciples had crossed the Lake of Galilee, they come to a region where Jesus heals a demoniac, who is encouraged to go home to his family and tell them what the Lord has done. When Jesus goes back across the lake, back to his home town, among those of his own family he indirectly confesses he himself as a prophet without honor among his relatives. In between this matter of whether one is accepted or rejected by one's own folks at home, Mark tells us of two incidents that have this in common: twelve years. A woman is healed after she has suffered for twelve years, and a girl who was twelve years of age is raised from the dead. Also, the catchword "daughter" links the two miracles concerned.

The home folk and twelve years

- A. After people pleaded for Jesus to leave their country when the demoniac was healed, the demoniac begged to go with Jesus. Yet Jesus told him to go *home* to his *family* and tell what the Lord had done. All who heard him were *amazed* (5:1-20).

- B. On the other side of the lake; Jesus heals a woman who had been subject to bleeding for *twelve years* (5:21-34). Jesus says, "*Daughter,* your faith has saved you."

- B. Jesus brings to life a synagogue ruler's *daughter*, who was *twelve years* of age (5:35-43).

1 Mirrors in Mark

> A. Jesus goes to his home town where he preaches in the local synagogue so that his hearers are *amazed* at his wisdom. Yet the amazement gives way to offence, leaving Jesus to say that only in his home town, among his *relatives* and in his own *home*, is he a prophet without honor (6:1–6).

Mark is unique in mirroring incidents to do with speaking and witnessing to one's own folk and in one's own house. Luke refers to the demoniac being sent home to testify (Matthew omits a reference to it), and Luke does not refer to the account of Jesus returning home where his own people and house are said not to honor him. Luke refers to Jesus' Twelve being vested with authority to go out as his delegates or apostles, after relating for us the stories about the bleeding woman and the dead girl. Mark comes back to the issue of testifying to one's own folk after relating the same kind of two stories in a beautiful balance typical of the structure of his gospel.

Mark provokes us as readers to consider the question of the appropriateness of testimony among one's own. The demoniac knows amazement among those who hear him when testifying. So too does Jesus (Mark uses two different words for amazement each time but they are usually translated simply as "amazement" in many translations). However, the amazement or dumbfoundedness gave way to offence when Jesus testified. Why? What was the difference between Jesus' testimony and that of the demoniac? Whatever concession of admiration was given to Jesus' wisdom and works turned into a trap, whereby what was palpable became finally denied in unbelief. A dark truth that Mark seems to desire us to see.

Matthew relates the incident of the rejection of Jesus at Nazareth but in a different context, not in the kind of symmetry Mark had in mind for his own gospel.

Only Mark tells us the dead girl was twelve years of age. It strongly suggests he was strengthening the link even more between the healing of the bleeding woman and the raising of the dead girl. It all spelt for a better memory of what took place when Jesus crossed the lake again. With the gospel story circulating as oral history, it aided memory. Yet, even the gospel story in written form was to be aided by the catchword "twelve."

Mirrors in Mark (and in other New Testament Writings)

1.1 RECOGNITION AND THE LOAVES (MARK 6:6B-56)

In this new panel Mark draws attention to the fact that Jesus' name had become well-known (v.14). The crowds swell around him, even to following him to desolate places. In a desolate place Jesus dismisses the crowd after the miracle of the loaves, and his disciples are tested in the howling wind on the lake. They are reminded of the loaves (v.52). Then, when they cross the lake, once more crowds mill around Jesus because they recognize him on account of his fame. So the inverted parallelism is taken up with the fame of Jesus and the matter of the loaves. The fame of Jesus (6:6b–29) leads to desired rest; the miracle of the loaves takes place; the disciples are found to be without faith through not understanding about the loaves; and Jesus disembarks at Gennesaret to find his fame has gone before him.

Recognition and the loaves

A. Jesus goes around the *villages* teaching. Herod learns of Jesus, as Jesus' fame had spread not only through his personal ministry, but through the apostles doing in the name of Jesus what he himself had been doing. The *fame* of Jesus troubled King Herod, as the ruler thought that Jesus was a reincarnation of John the Baptist whom he beheaded (6:6b–29).

B. Jesus feeds a crowd with five *loaves* and two fish (6:30–44).

B. The disciples of Jesus are said to be wrongly amazed at Jesus, fearing he was a ghost on the lake. They were chided, having hard hearts through not understanding the miraculous feeding of the crowd with five *loaves* (6:45–52).

A. At Gennesaret (as the original has it) and among the *villages* Jesus is *fully recognized*, "known full well, could not avoided being recognized, especially recognized" (6:53–56).

If one thinks in strict terms of catchwords and catchphrases, the action that Mark sees as giving rise to Herod being troubled by the fame of Jesus does not mirror the account to do with Jesus landing at Gennesaret and the crowds recognizing him full well. Still, the events flanking the action to do with the feeding of the five thousand men and the disciples' lack of understanding bear similarity in revolving around the fame of Jesus.

1 Mirrors in Mark

The mere length of this new panel may seem to go against accepting it as an inverted parallelism, but inverted parallelisms need not necessarily be of similar and of relative short length. This inverted parallelism carries two events that find Mark slowing down the flow of his gospel by dwelling on the two events in considerable detail. Comparing Mark with Matthew and Luke at this juncture, it is to be noticed that Mark goes into greater lengths to tell us about the death of John the Baptist and the mind of Herod, and to tell us of the feeding of the five thousand.

With respect to the crossing of the Lake by Jesus and his disciples after the miraculous feeding, it is Mark alone who tells us of the link between the loaves and Jesus walking on the lake—"The disciples were completely amazed, for they had not understood about the loaves; their hearts were hardened."

Mark appears to be consciously putting forward sets of mirrors similar in form to not only make his gospel memorable but to provoke thought in the serious reader each time, all this while proceeding to tell us of the words and works of Jesus from beginning to end.

1.J UNCLEAN PEOPLE AND FOREIGN SOIL (MARK 7:1-8:21)

We now reach the point of what is commonly known as The Retirement Ministry. As Jesus faced increasing hostility—particularly from the spiritual leaders of the day—it was a prudent thing and one of vision to retreat from the crowds and spend time teaching his disciples in the light of his oncoming death.

All three Synoptic writers adopt some of the material that doubtlessly had circulated at first as oral tradition and what was in accordance with Jesus' movements during the retirement ministry. In addition to catchwords, catchphrases, and other devices to bring to mind what Jesus had done and said, there was the common retelling of where Jesus went and what he did and said upon retreating from his opponents in the Pharisees and scribes, and going to territory outside Israel, before he eventually crossed the Jordan and headed south towards Jerusalem for the last time.

A look at a map of the retirement ministry helps one to realize how Jesus' movements could well have been recalled by those acquainted with the geography of Israel.[6] Not only his movements but the events of the time.

---

6. For a Retirement Map see Hendriksen's *The Gospel of Luke*, 491

Mirrors in Mark (and in other New Testament Writings)

In this new set of mirrors we find Jesus speaks to the Pharisees and the teachers of the law about what constitutes being clean or unclean. Then upon leaving them, Jesus heals the daughter of a woman on foreign soil, followed by a healing of a deaf and dumb man who was presumably a Gentile as well, followed in turn by Jesus speaking to his disciples on the heels of feeding the four thousand about the uncleanness of the Pharisees.

Unclean people and foreign soil

A. Pharisees and some of the scribes were carping at Jesus because his disciples ate bread with *unclean hands*. He in turn criticizes his opponents, reminding them uncleanness is an inward thing. When his disciples ask Jesus about his parable, he chides them with: "Are you so *dull*? Do you not *see*...?" (7:1–23).

B. Jesus attempts to keep his presence a secret in Tyre's vicinity but a distressed woman *begs* Jesus to heal her daughter (7:24–30).

B. In the region of the Decapolis people *beg* Jesus to cure a deaf and dumb man. After the healing—performed away from the crowd—Jesus commands the healing be kept a secret (7:31–37).

A. Jesus tells his disciples to beware of *the leaven* of the Pharisees and that of Herod after the feeding of the four thousand. They think he is obliquely criticizing them in the boat, and he then asks: "Do you still not *see* or *understand*?" (8:1–21).

Some catchwords do not strictly match up in the mirrors above as based on the original language, but they remain as catchwords all the same. For instance, *yeast* and *unclean* are dissimilar in word form, yet the Jews of Jesus' day would have connected the two, since at Passover time yeast was to be removed from Jewish houses, symbolizing the removal of uncleanness. Also, the two words translated as "beg," in connection with both miracles performed outside of Israel, are dissimilar in form but they can be both rendered as 'beg', thus aligning the two miracles in the sense that there was an urgent request both times for Jesus to heal.

The theme of uncleanness actually pervades the whole of this chiasmus, as Gentiles were regarded as unclean people by the Jews. Note that Pharisees would wash their hands after visiting the marketplace where direct or indirect contact with Gentiles may have been made (7:4). It is ironic that those who regarded themselves as clean were actually unclean according to Jesus, and ironic that Jesus would leave the Pharisees and go beyond Israel's territory to heal two who would have been regarded as unclean by the Pharisees.

When Jesus warns his own about the yeast of the Pharisees, some light can be shed on what he meant in what mirrors the warning in Jesus' earlier word to the Pharisees (7:1–24). What constituted yeast? Hypocrisy (7:6), and a leaning on foolish traditions at the expense of drawing near to God in their hearts (7:6–13).

1.K HALF-SEEING AND SUFFERING (MARK 8:22–9:10)

It may seem Procrustean to have as a mirror for the Transfiguration (9:2–10) the event of the healing of the blind man at Bethsaida (8:22–26), as there is no exact catchword or catchphrase to justify that kind of mirror, and there are no words that may carry the same meaning (as in the case of "beg" in 7:24–37). Then, in what way do the two events of the healing of the blind man and the Transfiguration mirror one another? I suggest there is a kind of parable in the healing of the blind man to reflect what occurred later on the Mount of Transfiguration.

Still recovering from the gentle chiding they received from Jesus on the boat journey, the disciples enter a critical time for understanding the nature of Jesus' ministry. They must learn that while he displays great power to do the miraculous, Jesus had come to suffer. They must learn to listen to Jesus. They had to learn to look—for instance, look beyond the miraculous feedings referred to when on the lake with him. They must learn to listen about what lies ahead for both Jesus and themselves, hence Jesus' clear prediction of his death and the call on all to take up their cross as well.

Half-seeing and suffering

A. Jesus is sought in order to heal a blind man at Bethsaida. He leads the blind man to outside the village, where he heals him in two stages. At Jesus' first "attempt," the blind man does not *see clearly*—people merely look like trees to him. The blind man is told to *suppress* the news of his restoration (8:22–26).

> B. Once Peter confesses Jesus is the Christ, the disciples are told "the Son of Man must suffer," and will be killed. This is viewed as *the will of God* (8:27–33).
>
> > B. All of Jesus' hearers are called on to deny themselves and "take up his cross and follow me." This is viewed as a *necessity*, just as Jesus' death is to be (8:34–9:1).
>
> A. Jesus leads Peter, James, and John up a mountain, where the four will be alone. There Jesus is dazzlingly transfigured. Peter speaks before he thinks, *not knowing what to say*, being frightened, as were the other two privileged disciples. Upon descending the mountain, the disciples are ordered to *suppress* the matter of what they had seen (9:2–10).

In a broad sense I suggest we link "Do you still not see and understand?" (8:18) with Jesus asking the purblind man "Do you see anything?" For as yet the disciples not only failed to comprehend how Jesus could care for them in the boat when they had no bread, but also failed to "see" what lay in the future for Jesus, though it was confessed that Jesus was the Christ.

Although Peter for one confessed Jesus to be the Christ (v.29), he could not see that Jesus must suffer and be killed. He challenges Jesus on the point. He "half-saw" that Jesus is the Christ. He must completely see: Jesus is to be the suffering Christ, as it was in the plan of God. Not only that, but Peter (and all of us) must see that by necessity we are to take up our own cross and follow Christ if we are to share in the coming glory. On the Mount of Transfiguration, Peter does not "see" as he ought: he desires the glory of the kingdom to linger instead of going the way of suffering, hence the need for the Voice from the cloud: "This is My Son, whom I love. Listen to him."

1.L JESUS THE CHRIST AND ARGUMENTS (MARK 9:11–41)

According to Mark, after Jesus comes down from the Mount of Transfiguration, the disciples wonder if Jesus is the Christ, when it seemed that Elijah had not preceded him as expected. Then there are two incidents where Jesus asked what was virtually the same question, followed in Mark by a clear reference to Jesus being the Christ through self-acknowledgement.

1 Mirrors in Mark

Jesus the Christ and arguments

A. When the Kingdom came with power in transfiguration (9:1) so that Jesus was plainly seen to be the Christ, the disciples ask the question: "Why do the teachers of the law say that *Elijah must come first?*" (9:11–13).

   B. At the foot of the mountain a large crowd mills around Jesus' other disciples, who have the teachers of the law arguing with them. Jesus asks, "*What are you arguing with them about?*" (9:14–32)

   B. At Capernaum Jesus asks his disciples, "*What were you arguing about on the road?*" (9:14–37)

A. When John tells Jesus that he had dissuaded someone from casting out demons in Jesus' name—someone who was not "one of us"—Jesus tells John he was in the wrong. Such a person is for Jesus. "Anyone who (even) gives a cup of water in my name because you belong to *Christ* will certainly not lose his reward." (9:38–41)

Admittedly, the actual name of Christ is not referred to when the disciples ask Jesus why it was said Elijah must come first, but it is obvious the three had "Christ" in mind, Jesus' kingship being evidenced on the mount.

With respect to similar questions following one another in Mark, we see the author making what is a deliberate attempt to bring into juxtaposition two rather similar questions. It suggests a mnemonic device is being employed but, in addition, such juxtaposition calls on the reader to exercise considerable reflection as to different arguments that may come into play in relationship to Jesus. Actually, the first word for arguing has more to do with "dispute," and the second one more to do with "discourse"—but arguing all the same in both cases.

Mark is alone in not only juxtaposing these almost identical questions, but also he alone has Jesus asking on the very way to Capernaum "What were you arguing about on the road?" Matthew and Luke omit the question for the same event.

To mirror what transpired on descending the mount, Mark touches on the occasion to do with "the strange exorcist," and he alone among the Synoptics tells us the word "Christ" fell from Jesus' own lips then (v.41). It may seem strange to view the familiar term "Christ" as a catchword and as reflecting "Elijah must come first," but on only three occasions according to Mark did the word "Christ" come from Jesus' own lips. In the incident of "the strange exorcist" it is the one that applies most directly of all to Jesus being the promised Christ.

Moreover, another possible link between 9:11–13 and 9:38–41 lies in the concept of suffering. The Christ is to suffer (9:12), and many a disciple will too, for why should a disciple be desiring a cup of water unless he is in extremity and has been denied a cup by others who oppose him? Even the service of Jesus' disciples is considered as well as Jesus' own in Mark's unique work—service in suffering both for Jesus and his disciples.

1.M ENTERING THE KINGDOM AND ACCEPTANCE AT HOME (MARK 9:42–10:34)

On the heels of the teaching about those who are not against us (9:38–41), Mark would have us consider any who may be against the cause of Jesus in the sense of anyone causing "one of these little ones who believe in me to sin." As these words quickly follow on the heels of those about any humble servant of his giving a brother or sister a cup of water, it appears "these little ones" are childlike adult believers as well as children, being like "the strange exorcist," made to stumble because they are discouraged by the likes of other disciples who dissuade them from doing things in Jesus' name. That the "little ones" may include actual children seems to be borne out by the text of 9:33–37.

The subject of causing "these little ones who believe in me to sin" centers around the grave matter of sinning to the degree one will not enter the Kingdom of God. "The Kingdom of God" is here the catchphrase that links up with the story of the rich young man.

In between the two episodes to do with entry into the Kingdom of God are two that do not have either a catchword or a catchphrase but have a natural link in that "divorce" and "children" are frequently inseparable issues.

Entering the Kingdom and acceptance at Home

A. Jesus warns against causing *little ones* who believe in him to sin. He says that dismemberment of parts of the body is little to pay if offending little ones prevents us from *entering the kingdom of God* (9:42–50).

> B. Jesus meets his opponents head-on about *divorce* by reminding them of God's original design for marriage (10:1–12).
>
> B. Jesus blesses *children*, perhaps in the house where he was staying. See v.10. (10:13–16).
>
> A. Jesus challenges a rich man to give his wealth to the poor and follow him. When the rich man's face falls, Jesus says to his disciples, "*Children, how hard it is to enter the kingdom of God!*" (10:17–31).

There is much more distance in Matthew and Luke between the words about offence against "little ones" and the account of the rich man than there is in Mark. Only the two passages about marriage, divorce and children separate the things to do with entering the Kingdom of God as Mark sees it. It suggests Mark has set up mirrors to draw close attention to much of what is entailed in entering the Kingdom of God.

If the words about offence and the story of the rich man are connected, we note the rich man is not "a little one" who believes. He has grown to be an adult, grown to glue himself to wealth—as children do not—so that he could not be numbered among those whom Jesus calls "children." It is unique to Mark that the disciples who had forsaken all to follow Jesus are called "children" when he speaks of the difficulty of the rich entering the kingdom.

1.N GOING AHEAD AND FOLLOWING, AND THE TWO REQUESTS (MARK 10:32–11:11)

The movements of Jesus during his retirement ministry, and his retreat from the opponents referred to in 7:1–23, were bound together rather easily in the minds of those acquainted with the topography of Israel and her neighbors in early times, but this did not deter Mark from using catchwords and catchphrases to mark the retirement ministry.

Now, Jesus' retirement ministry is behind him and we find Jesus and his disciples making their way up to Jerusalem for the final time. Actually, Mark has virtually nothing up to this point about Jesus ever being in Jerusalem. He had thrown great emphasis on Jesus' ministry in Galilee at the expense of saying anything about any journeys to Jerusalem. The Galilean Ministry threw no visits to Jerusalem into any relief—well-nigh into nonexistence, in fact—in order to make most dramatic the entry of Christ into

Jerusalem to die in accordance with the divine plan, and his opponents' evil intention to murder him.

Jesus goes up to Judea and Jerusalem via Perea, the region across the Jordan. All that takes place according to 10:1–52 transpires across the Jordan.

Yet, in light of what is mirrored in Mark we traverse into the passage containing what is commonly known as The Triumphal Entry (11:1–11).

Going ahead and following, and the two requests

A. *Going up to Jerusalem*, Jesus *goes ahead* of everyone else, leaving the disciples astonished and *those who followed* afraid. Jesus takes the Twelve aside to warn them of his impending death (10:32–34).

B. James and John have a request. Jesus asks them, "*What do you want me to do for you?*" (10:35–42).

B. A blind man at Jericho beseeches the Son of David to have mercy on him. Jesus asks him, "*What do you want me to do for you?*" (10:46–52).

A. Jesus and those with him *approach Jerusalem*. Preparations are made for Jesus to ride on a donkey into the city. He is hailed as the Davidic king. Those who *go ahead* and those *who follow* shout in acclamation that Jesus is the Davidic king to bring in the Kingdom (11:1–11).

Mark alone refers to Jesus going ahead of everyone else when going up to Jerusalem, as well as being alone among the Synoptics to record the amazement of the disciples and the fear for Jesus among the rest who followed. Only Matthew and Mark place and include one after the other the accounts of James and John's request and the healing of Bartimaeus. Both also have Jesus asking James and John and Bartimaeus the similar question, but the uniqueness of Mark lies in the fact that both the account of the brothers and the healing of Bartimaeus serve as midpoints in a chiasmus that have as their flanks the matter of *going ahead* of Jesus and *following* (as shown above). Matthew refers to the crowds going ahead of Jesus and following him when he makes his triumphant entry just as Mark does, but he omits reference to the going ahead and following at the time of Jesus' prediction of his death.

Even "Jerusalem" in itself is a catchword in Mark, for as a word it appears far less frequently in his gospel than perhaps expected. With the term "Jerusalem" each time being accompanied with *going up* and *approaching*, it becomes most memorable—Mark depicting graphically the tension of entering the city from which Jesus' opponents had gone up to Galilee more than once to ply him with questions poised to poison his popularity.

1.0 ATTEMPTING TO ARREST JESUS, THE QUESTION OF BELIEF (MARK 11:12–12:12)

Jesus arrived in Jerusalem, went to the temple and then stayed the night at Bethany. Next day, on the way to the temple, he cursed a fig tree. Within the temple he cleared it of the profiteers and their means of despicable commerce. The chief priests and scribes became bent on killing Jesus.

The successful cursing of the fig tree served for Jesus' disciples as a lesson in belief but, in returning to Jerusalem and the temple the next day, belief of another degree was voiced by Jesus when his opponents challenged him about authority to clear the temple. A piercing parable caused his opponents' enmity and frustration to be aroused with similar intensity to that when he had cleared the temple.

Attempting to arrest Jesus, the question of belief

A. After Jesus cleared the temple and called it the house of prayer for all nations but that it had been made a den of robbers, *the chief priests and scribes heard this and began looking for a way to kill him, for they feared him, because the whole crowd was amazed at his teaching* (11:12–18).

B. Once Peter had observed that the fig tree which Jesus cursed had withered, Jesus draws a lesson from the effective curse by telling his disciples to have faith in God without doubting, to *believe* when asking for something in prayer (11:19–25).

B. When Jesus was asked by what authority he cleared the temple and taught what he did, he questioned his opponents about John's baptism, and when they hesitated to answer as to whether or not they regarded John's baptism was of heaven, hesitation arose from being asked the question, "Why did you not *believe* John the Baptist?" (11:26–33).

A. The reaction to Jesus' parable about the tenants and the vineyard on the part of the chief priests, the scribes and the elders proved they knew he had spoken the parable against them, therefore *they were looking for a way to arrest him, but they were afraid of the crowd* (12:1–12).

It is Mark who refers to the similar murderous reaction of Jesus' opponents both after the temple was cleared and after telling of the parable of the tenants. Each of the episodes mirror one another therefore, lending to the consistent style of inverted parallelism Mark adopts for his unique gospel.

As for the passages to do with the lesson to be learnt from the cursing of the fig tree and that of Jesus' displaying authority at the temple, Matthew and Mark both refer to "belief." The difference with Mark, of course, is that the similar matters form the midpoints of a chiasmus that has an introduction and end of wording quite identical to sum up the murderous reaction to Jesus.

1.P LORDSHIP, ERROR AND RIGHT (MARK 12:13–40)

Jesus' opponents were seeking to arrest him, and it would appear they thought that before they arrested him, they would make a fool of him with tricky questions so as to expose his apparent authority and so that he lost his grip on the people. Then it would be easier to arrest him.

The first question in a bid to trap Jesus came from Pharisees and Herodians, who in flattery asked him about what one owes to God while acknowledging the lordship of Caesar. The second one engaged the Sadducees with Jesus over belief in resurrection life. Jesus branded the Sadducees' agnosticism as a great error, a bad mistake. Overhearing the debate about resurrection life, and noticing Jesus gave a good answer, a teacher of the law was soon commended for a wise answer he gave to what he regarded as rightly said by Jesus. Lastly, Jesus throws a question at the teachers of the law about the lordship of David's Greater Son, and it is presumed they could not answer it. Their lives were too bound up with hypocrisy to understand.

Lordship, error and right

- A. The Pharisees and the Herodians try to set Jesus up at first with flattery and, even though he knew their *hypocrisy*, he escaped the trap behind the question, showing he was no subversive figure. He acknowledges a circumscribed *lordship* to Caesar so that it becomes right to pay taxes— a matter the Herodians are left to ponder— showing he was no subversive political figure. He acknowledges what one owes to God (12:13–17).

  - B. When Jesus is tested on the subject of the resurrection, Mark records that Jesus said of the Sadducees, "*You are badly mistaken!*" (12:18–27).

  - B. Noticing that Jesus answered the Sadducees well, one of the teachers wished to have it confirmed that Jesus was a worthy teacher and asked him concerning the greatest commandment. The teacher's response to Jesus' answer was a response that had Jesus see the teacher *answering wisely* (12:28–34).

- A. After being grilled in order to trap him, Jesus throws up a counter-question in the temple courts. He asks how David could call Christ *Lord* if he is said to be his Son. While teaching, he warns against being deceived by the teachers' religiosity, stating amongst other things that only *for a show* they make lengthy prayers (12:35–40).

When confronted by the Pharisees and the Herodians, Jesus seems compelled to enter the arena where the lordship of Caesar is pitted against the lordship of God. The counterpoint to this lies in the question he later poses concerning David's Son, whom the scribes believed would be the Messiah: How can the Christ be his Son as well as his Lord? The question is followed with a condemnation levelled at the teachers of the law, which condemnation included making long prayers for show or pretense. Hypocrisy and pretense, though not the same words originally, both carry the idea of a false or misleading appearance.

Mark is alone among the Synoptics in both recording "You are badly mistaken" and "Jesus saw that he answered wisely" (vv. 27, 34). The Sadducees were badly mistaken, while a certain teacher of the Mosaic Law could answer wisely. Such a contrast serves to pit one response against the other and should cause the reader to explore the reasons and the rationale behind each response. Once again, Mark is found through the chiastic structure of his gospel to see another layer or two all along, so that comparisons and contrasts draw us into delving beyond what requires more than a cursory reading of his sacred writing.

1.Q WOMEN GIVING MUCH, KNOWING AND NOT KNOWING THE DAY (MARK 12:41–14:9)

Like Luke, Mark follows the reference to the teachers of the law devouring widows' houses with the record of the incident concerning the poor widow contributing out of her poverty to the temple treasury (so that "widow" is a catchword employed by Mark and Luke for the same reason) but Mark, in his unique style, has as a counterpoise to that of the poor widow the incident of the woman who came with the expensive perfume and anointed Jesus' head with it. And in between the two incidents about the women, Mark records Jesus' Olivet Discourse, which can be divided into two parts: one that relates to what we know regarding the day of Christ's return, the other to what we do not know.

Women giving much, knowing and not knowing the Day

- A. The poor widow puts into the temple treasury only two small copper coins but according to Jesus her giving was to be greatly commended, as she *put in everything—all she had to live on* (12:41–44)

    - B. Jesus speaks of the signs that will signify the nearness of his second coming. The signs will be as certain as those that indicate the nearness of summer when fig trees put forward their leaves. Hence, says Jesus, " . . . when you see these things happening, *you know* that it is near" (13:1–31)

    - B. On the other hand, with respect to the exact day or hour, he says, "*You do not know* when that time will come" (13:32–36)

- A. When Jesus neared the time of his death, a woman with very expensive perfume in a jar broke the jar and poured the perfume on Jesus' head. Some caviled at what they believed was waste but according to Jesus *"she did what she could"* (14:1–9)

1 Mirrors in Mark

There is neither catchword nor catchphrase strictly linking the incidents concerning the two women, but obviously there is a mirroring of one incident in the other. It certainly provokes the observant reader to compare and contrast the two women, and to note the two kinds of giving that are equally acceptable. Both the poor and wealthy can be commended. Note also the roles of true observation and false observation to do with the passages about the two women.

Within the midpoints of the chiasmus, however, there is the simple catchword "know," —a common word perhaps but elevated to a high rank when one considers the day of Christ's return. What confusion there has been down the centuries about the distinction between what we can know and what we cannot know about Christ's return! Many theories can be jettisoned when we clearly perceive what is knowable and what is unknowable.

1.R THE BETRAYAL AND THE TWO CUPS (MARK 14:10–52)

In the next chiasmus the side-points or the flanks have to do with the betrayal of Jesus by Judas and the way he planned to hand Jesus over, while the midpoints center both on Jesus taking a cup and offering it to his disciples during his last Passover Feast and Jesus in the Garden of Gethsemane asking the Father, "Take this cup from me."

The betrayal and the two cups

- A. Judas Iscariot, one of the twelve, when he discovered the chief priests were delighted to hear he wished to betray Jesus, *watched for an opportunity to hand him over* (14:10–11)

- B. During the Passover Feast Jesus tells his disciples to "*Take the cup (from me),*" the cup that symbolized his blood of the covenant (14:12–31)

- B. In the garden Jesus in prayer agonizes over the cup of suffering he is to drink, momentarily wishing he did not have to do so: "*Take this cup from me.*" Yet, he submits to his Father's will (14:32–42).

- A. Judas, one of the twelve, appears in the garden, having worked out a good opportunity to effect the betrayal of Jesus. He *had given the*

Jewish authorities a signal by which Jesus would be apprehended (14:43–51).

While Judas Iscariot's name is well-known to us because of his infamy, he is rarely referred to in Mark, that is, until he decides to betray Jesus. His name then becomes a significant catchword to link 14:10–11 with 14:43–51, with each passage occupied with Judas' opportunity to betray Jesus. Each time he is referred to as "one of the twelve" in order to underline the gravity of his deed.

Of the Synoptic gospel writers Mark and Matthew show a more direct link between the episode of the cup of the Passover Feast Jesus offers his disciples and that of the cup the Father is calling on him to drink when in the Garden of Gethsemane. Because of his economy and brevity with words, Mark ever so slightly speeds up his narrative more than Matthew so that the link between the two cups is apparent. Teasing out the many contrasts and comparisons that may be made between the offer of the Passover cup and the offer of the Father's cup can lead to deeper insights into the remembrance of the ransom required for salvation.

1.S ILL-TREATMENT, DENIAL AND CONFESSION (14:53–15:20)

In this the second last of the simple inverted parallelisms of Mark's gospel, flanking the passages to do with Peter's denial of Jesus and Jesus' confession to the danger of losing his life is the subject each time of ill-treatment—ill-treatment of Jesus at the hands of the Jews and then at the hands of the Romans.

Ill-treatment, denial and confession

A. When Jesus stood trial before the Sanhedrin, it was Jesus' admission to being the Christ, the Son of the Blessed, that caused the Sanhedrin to pronounce him worthy of death. At that, they *struck him* with their fists, and *spat on him*, insisting he prophesy after blindfolding him. Then guards took him and beat him (14:53–65).

B. Peter *denies* Jesus in the courtyard (14:66–72)

B. When Pilate asks Jesus if he is King of the Jews, He replies, *"Yes, it is as you say"* (15:1–15).

A. Jesus is led away to the palace to suffer at the hands of the Roman soldiers who, among other things, *strike him* on the head with a staff and *spit on him* (15:16–20).

Mark says very little about "the trial before the trial" that transpired on the eve of Jesus' arrest, so that Jesus' confession of being the Christ that evening is not recorded by Mark. He records Peter's denial before going into detail about what transpired in the morning, when Jesus made "a good confession" before both the Sanhedrin and Pilate. In Matthew and Mark the episode of Peter's denial is surrounded by Jesus' confession in the morning before the Sanhedrin and then by his confession before Pontius Pilate.

The shortness of Mark's gospel allows him to speed up the narrative so that any comparison or contrast that may be made between the Jews' ill-treatment of Jesus and that by the Romans can be more easily discerned. Once attempts at comparison and contrast are made, what perhaps first appeared as a simple gospel for quick digestion may not appear so simple after all.

The catchwords "struck" and "spat" are far more apparent in the shortest gospel of all, but in the passages about Peter's denial and Jesus' confession strictly a catchword is lacking, and yet the shortness of the gospel makes the contrast between denial and confession quite striking when viewed side by side.

1.T BUILDING THE TEMPLE IN THREE DAYS, THE CENTURION (15:21–16:8)

In the last of the inverted parallelisms in Mark, as based on the recurring A-B-B-A pattern, we arrive at an appropriate conclusion for a gospel that states as an introduction: "The beginning of the gospel about Jesus Christ, the Son of God." In the last of the parallelisms, Jesus is seen first as crucified, as appearing to fail to fulfil his words about destroying the temple and building it again in three days, but he actually fulfils prophecy, Mark showing somewhat cryptically it was so. According to Mark, the Roman centurion is a key figure for proof Jesus died, this in addition to the centurion uttering a remarkable confession.

Mirrors in Mark (and in other New Testament Writings)

Building the temple in three days, the centurion

> A. Among the insults hurled at Jesus when he hangs upon the cross is this: *"So! You, who are going to destroy the temple and build it in three days, come down from the cross and save yourself!"* (15:21–32).
>
> > B. When Jesus cries out and breathes his last, *the centurion*, who stood in front of Jesus, heard his cry and, noticing how he died, exclaimed, "Surely this man was the Son of God!" (15:33–42).
> >
> > B. It was *the centurion* who was summoned by Pilate for confirmation of Jesus' death. Upon the centurion certifying Jesus' death, Joseph is given the body (15:42–47).
>
> A. *When the Sabbath was over, that is, on the third day according to Jewish reckoning, Jesus, whose "temple" had been crucified, rises from the dead.*16:1–8).

The connection between the passage concerning Jesus' death and the account of his resurrection, as Mark has it, is rather cryptic, if we consider that he has left no record that Jesus ever said anything about destroying the temple and building it again. The insult thrown at Jesus while dying (15:29) is also mentioned by Matthew, but neither author records that Jesus asserted he would destroy the temple and rebuild it. John alone tells of the occasion when Jesus uttered the claim. The cryptic nature of it is captured by Matthew and Mark merely stating what the blasphemers said of Jesus, and obviously misinterpreting what he once stated. Cryptically, without explaining what Jesus meant by the word, Mark shrouds the answer to the riddle somewhat when he states in "the mirror" Jesus arose on the third day after his body (the temple) had been destroyed.

It is Mark alone who refers twice to the centurion in the story of the crucifixion, and he alone refers to two actions performed by the Roman: that of crying out "Surely this man was the Son of God," and that of confirming to Pilate that Jesus was definitely dead so that Joseph's request was then granted. The two actions of the centurion follow quite closely in the Markan account and make him a prominent figure in the final hours of that dark day.

While Matthew speaks of the Roman centurion and the accompanying soldiers exclaiming "Surely this is the Son of God" upon actually seeing the earthquake as Jesus was dying, Mark is silent about the earthquake and its effect on those Romans. Why? Mark saw it sufficient to record the centurion's confession in the light of how Jesus died. It appears that more than the earthquake accounted for the staggering confession, ascribing deity to Jesus a man, and a dying man at that.

While Joseph of Arimathea emerges as a prominent figure when it comes to giving Jesus a respectful burial, more than one Markan scholar has Joseph overshadowing the centurion too much. More attention needs to be drawn to the centurion's role in confirming Jesus was dead, with all that it implied.

Jesus definitely died. Then again, he definitely rose from the grave. The Temple had been rebuilt.

The longer ending of Mark (16:9–20)

There appears no chiastic structure in what is commonly known as the longer ending of Mark, which is regarded by many scholars as non-Markan, and seen as a weak attempt to complete what Mark wrote—because the gospel seems to end too abruptly.

A lack of chiastic structure in the longer ending does not mean that on these grounds alone the ending is to be rejected, but it may help to substantiate the argument that the ending is spurious and non-Markan.

The gospel probably ended with the wonder of Christ's resurrection, thus the abrupt ending at 16:8. For Mark had written a gospel about Jesus Christ, *the Son of God*. It would do us well to re-live the amazement—indeed, the bewilderment—at learning he has arisen.

2

Mirrors in Romans

WITH GOOD REASON ROMANS can be viewed essentially as comprising two large parts: part one extending from 1:1 to 6:23, part two from 7:7 to the end. The two parts have as their bridge 7:1–6.

A good number of scholars have all divided the great book up into two parts, but in a different way from the above. They do so by suggesting 1:1 to 11:36 covers doctrine, while the Christian way of life is spelt out from 12:1 on. F.F. Bruce gives all of 1:16–11:36 such a title as "The Gospel According to Paul" and 12:1 on as "The Christian Way of Life."[1] Another, in a somewhat similar vein, calls 1:18 to 11:36 "The Doctrinal Treatise," and 12:1 to 15:13 "The Practical Treatise.[2] "Exhortation—The Will of God Revealed" is another suggested title for 12:1 and beyond, claiming that it is only then that the apostle is dealing with the issue of "How should a saved man walk?"[3] Other scholars also could be quoted as seeing Romans 12:1–15:33 in terms of describing the Christian way of life, and its preceding material in terms of Paul writing about the Gospel and the need of lost men to find salvation in Christ.

David Seccombe, in his commentary "Dust to Destiny," does not dissect and split Romans in half as others do. Instead, he lists 31 divisions in all and in a way that more or less suggests the Gospel of Paul only covers Romans 1–6, while 7–16 has to do with counsel for believers. It is interesting that Seccombe's division 17 "Beyond the Law" (7:1–13) is approximately

1. F.F. Bruce, *Romans*, 67-68
2. Godet, *Romans*, 63-64
3. McClain, *Romans*, 9-10

the center of his divisions. A claim can be made for Seccombe having a more accurate insight into the structure of Romans, seeing Romans 7 on as counsel for believers.

Romans can be made into a large chiasmus, with the following form of inverted parallelism: A B C D E F G H G F E D C B A. Romans 1:1–6:23 can fall into seven divisions. Romans 7:1–6 forms the bridge to the other seven divisions that cover 7:7–16:27. While no divisions for Romans will ever be watertight, the above inverted parallelism takes into some consideration not only how men are saved but acknowledges the appreciable space that is given to the status and the stimulation spelt out in the letter for those who are already saved. The first seven divisions of Romans 1 to 6 mirror the second lot of divisions of Romans 7:7 to 16 insofar as there is a spelling out firstly in Romans of what is true of an unsaved man as opposed to what secondly is true of a saved man. That is, Paul employs similar mirror-like words to contrast saint with sinner. For example, Paul speaks of the degraded body and the depraved mind of the sinner in the first division and, in considering the body and mind of the saint in the second and reflective division, the apostle tells his readers to offer their bodies to God and transform their minds.

Moreover, before "crossing the bridge" (7:1–6) the word of exhortation is not as prominent as it is afterwards, since "before the bridge" the saints are being first reminded of what they were, and the state all sinners are in. Romans was written for the Roman church and, while it appeals to sinners, it is fore-mostly addressing believers, consequently "The Christian way of life" is referred to even before "crossing the bridge," with the status of believers already coming into view in Romans 4–6 especially. The Christian way of life becomes even plainer still at Romans 7:7, at the point where the apostle begins outlining the believers' way of life and does so with increasing exhortation. It is hoped all this becomes clear through the suggested chiasmus, as Paul moves from what we believers once were and what we now are in terms of status, moving to what we now ought to be in terms of sanctification.

2. ROMANS

Salvation for Jew and Gentile

- A. Prophecy, obedience, benediction (1:1–7)
  - B. Ambition, hindrance, obligation (1:8–17)
    - C. Divine wrath, body and mind, passing judgment (1:18–2:29)
      - D. Jews' advantage, no difference, children of promise (3:1–4:25)
        - E. Hope, glory, God's love in Christ, the Holy Spirit (5:1–21)
          - F. Slaves, mortal bodies, death to sin (6:1–14)
            - G. Thanks for freedom, and slavery to righteousness (6:15–23)
              - H. The analogy of marriage (7:1–6)
            - G. Thanks for freedom, and slavery to righteousness (7:7–25)
          - F. Slaves, mortal bodies, death to sin (8:1–17)
        - E. Hope, glory, God's love in Christ, the Holy Spirit (8:18–39)
      - D. Jews' advantage, no difference, children of promise (9:1–11:36)
    - C. Divine wrath, body and mind, passing judgment (12:1–15:13)
  - B. Ambition, hindrance, obligation (15:14–33)
- A. Prophecy, obedience, benediction (16:1–27)

2.A PROPHECY, OBEDIENCE, BENEDICTION (1:1–7)

Thanks to the European Reformation the doctrine of justification by faith was recovered as inspired by Romans, but Romans is not merely about justification by faith. The great purpose of Paul's monumental letter is unveiled as one might expect in the letter's preface. The letter promises to spell out the long-awaited news of salvation, which had to do with God's Son. Note in the preface, with respect to the gospel, the focus on the Davidic human nature, Christ's resurrection, with the Lordship of Christ setting out to win complete obedience through faith among the Gentiles. It is a healthy thing to trace such themes in Romans, to know how the letter satisfies what is stressed in the preface.

Prophecy, obedience, benediction

Paul declares *the promised gospel*. He received both apostleship and grace in order to call *all the Gentiles to obedience* that comes by faith. For the called of Rome he seeks the benediction of *grace* and *peace*.

2.B AMBITION, HINDRANCE, OBLIGATION (1:8-17)

Paul thanks God for the good report he had received about the Roman believers. His desire to visit the Romans is characterized by three inner driving forces, expressed as: "I long to see you . . . ," "I am obligated . . . ", "I am not ashamed . . . " He talks of reaching Greeks and non-Greeks (uncultured people), and also Jews and Gentiles.

Ambition, hindrance, obligation

Paul hopes God's will shall enable him to get to Rome, as *he is eager* to preach the gospel there, but thus far he had been *prevented from doing so*. His ambition is reflected in saying "*I long to see you,*" "*I am obligated*"," *I am not ashamed.*" The gospel is *first for the Jew*.

2.C DIVINE WRATH, BODY AND MIND, PASSING JUDGMENT (1:18-2:29)

The good news is such because God's wrath is manifest in the world. Among other things, its manifestation is evidenced in people universally possessing degraded bodies and depraved minds.

As sinners, there is no room to judge other sinners, as we all sin and do similar things. Passing judgment does not help us escape a further manifestation of God's wrath when his righteous judgment will be fully revealed in the Day of Christ. In the reception of the gospel the Jews are primarily privileged, but the unbelievers among them will be severely judged on the last great Day.

Mirrors in Mark (and in other New Testament Writings)

Divine wrath, body and mind, passing judgment

God's wrath is revealed from heaven on all godlessness and wickedness. By rejecting the evidence of God's existence, power and nature, people end up with *the degrading of their bodies and a depraved mind*. There is no consolation in *passing judgment on someone else*, as we all do similar things. God's kindness is designed to have us—both Jew and Gentile—repent. Jews *break the law—circumcision* is valid only if the law is observed. *Praise* is valid only among Jews who are so inwardly.

2.D THE JEWS' ADVANTAGE, NO DIFFERENCE, CHILDREN OF PROMISE (3:1–4:25)

Even though not all Jews have faith, there is an advantage in being a Jew. At such an early stage of the letter the advantage is not fully spelt out. The present emphasis lies in establishing the fact that everyone—both Jew and Gentile—have sinned. The proof lies not only in observation of people's conduct (Romans 1–2) but in the verdict of Scripture. Both Jew and Gentile have alike sinned and alike, upon believing, are justified through Christ's blood. David and Abraham—great fathers of the Jewish faith—are seen to be believers in God's righteousness and not their own, in line with what is sought for belief in Christ. And all who believe, as Abraham did, are his offspring.

The Jews' advantage, no difference, children of promise

What advantage was there in being Jews? Much in every way! First of all, they were entrusted with the very words of God. Still, *according to Scripture, Jews and Gentiles alike* have sinned. *There is no difference*, for all have sinned. *Abraham's offspring* are children of the promise. *Belief that Jesus was raised from the dead* means salvation.

2.E HOPE, GLORY, GOD'S LOVE IN CHRIST, THE HOLY SPIRIT (5:1–21)

"We have peace" (5:1) fits in better than the hortative "Let us have peace" (a possible alternative reading), as the context suggests Paul is at pains to tell believers of their status before God, pointing to the signs of our standing.

He proceeds to write of the hope of glory we have, and how suffering can be rejoiced in since the love of God is manifested through it.

At this stage of the apostle's letter the Holy Spirit is mentioned for the first time, when Paul mounts up the evidence of our sound status before God, who in his love sent Christ to justify us and save us from condemnation. All is working out well for those who believe.

Hope, glory, God's love in Christ, the Holy Spirit

We rejoice *in the hope of glory*, knowing that *suffering* produces that hope which stems from God's love by *the Holy Spirit*. We are to understand God's love was manifested too through Christ's love that spares us of *condemnation* and grants us *justification*.

2.F SLAVES, MORTAL BODIES, DEATH TO SIN (6:1-14)

Shall we exploit the grace of God by sinning? How can we, if we have died to sin? We have been baptized in Christ. Being saturated by his person, we therefore die to sin as he did. For this reason we who were slaves to sin and are now dead to sin are to count ourselves dead to sin. Sin is not to reign in our mortal bodies.

Slaves, mortal bodies, death to sin

Through God in Christ we are no longer *slaves*—slaves to sin. We are to *count ourselves dead to sin* so that it does not reign in our *mortal bodies*.

2.G THANKS RENDERED FOR FREEDOM, AND SLAVERY TO RIGHTEOUSNESS (6:15-23)

The accent is on thankfulness to God, since we are no more slaves to sin, but slaves to righteousness. This word about slavery to righteousness is a new note. Dying to sin and being set free is something to triumph in, though it seems to be a negative action to a degree. Positively we are slaves to righteousness.

Thanks rendered for freedom, and slavery to righteousness

Thanks be to God for now we are slaves to righteousness, slaves to God himself.

2.H THE ANALOGY OF MARRIAGE (7:1-6)

Frequently in an inverted parallelism—such as we suggest for Romans and such as frequently found in the Old Testament—the midpoint can be the heart of the purpose in its formation, that is, it may feature what is central to the message being conveyed.

It may well be debatable that Romans 7:1-6 is the core of Romans, and that it is the most crucial passage in the letter addressed to the Roman believers. Yet, it touches on the ever-occurring matter in Romans of the law of God. "One might become frustrated at the amount of attention given to the law in Romans," yet, says David Seccombe: "For Paul the Jew it was the center of his life and culture, the center of his understanding of God and his world, and his daily preoccupation as a Pharisee." We may add too that God's written law was not regarded purely as a Jewish matter according to Paul: It touched on the life of the Gentile as well. Paul is addressing believing Jew and Gentile in drawing on his analogy of marriage.

What is new in 7:1-7, and why is it pivotal to know? Is it mere repetition, or even a summary of all that had been stated thus far? To some degree there is little that is new. What is new? The concept of breaking free of God's law has the knack of arousing our passions to violate it. Paul held that we as believers have been freed of the force of our passions to violate that law. He claims we now serve in "the new way of the Spirit, and not in the old way of the written code."

On reflection this gives rise to a number of agonizing questions believers will have: "If it is true that I am freed of sinful passions, why do I still sin as a believer?" "Where is the victory I am supposed to have?" "Is there no place for the law now in a believer?"

While it can be said that Paul deals with the issue of sin ceasing to have dominion over the believer in 6:15-23, and then considers the proposition that the believer is not under the law here in 7:1-6, Paul proceeds to consider the matter of both sin and the law in the words following 7:1-6.

Too soon that which we have called "the bridge" of 7:1-6 may be passed over without realizing "the image of marriage is an important clue to the character of the life that lies in the realm beyond the law."[4] We have died to the law that "(we) might belong to another". Belonging to Christ moved John Owen the Puritan to say, "Every day is a wedding day." We belong to a dear Person and are not wedded to a written book of law. Yet, such a notion can be misunderstood, so that Paul goes to some length in much of what is left in his letter to show that the law comes alive in the sense of it not arousing sinful passion in those who believe but becomes the means of uniting us through the Spirit in reciprocal devotion to the Christ who loves us.

2.G THANKS RENDERED FOR FREEDOM AND SLAVERY TO RIGHTEOUSNESS (7:7-25)

We have crossed "the bridge." Or, to change the metaphor, we begin to view the reflections of 1:1–6:23. Like Alice in *Through the Looking Glass*, all is now seen in reverse.

At first sight it may seem we have no reflection of 6:15–23, because Paul is dealing with the struggle there is with sin under the law, and then the struggle with sin as a believer. Paul first speaks of being aroused to sin under the law and being conquered, but this was before he belonged to Christ (7:7–13). He proceeds to deal with the struggle with sin now that he belongs to Christ (7:14–25).

The prevailing view historically has been that 7:14–25 depicts the believer's struggle, and with good reason. Paul changes to present tense from verse 14 on. He will speak of what he does not want to do now that he believes in Christ. He speaks of delighting in God's law and appears to rejoice in a present victory, as believers do. Moreover, it would be strange if, in a letter such as this, and at this point of the letter, the agonizing struggle believers suffer through nagging sin was passed over in silence.

Thanks rendered for freedom and slavery to righteousness

Paul deeply grieves over the conflict between doing what he does not want to do and desiring to do what is good. He feels he is *sold as a slave to sin*. It is "leftover" sin that makes him feel helpless. The turmoil arises because in his inner being he delights in God's law. He cries out about his wretchedness

---

4. Seccombe, *Dust to Destiny* (commentary *on Romans)*, 120

but that cry is a longing for victory, which he knows will come. Therefore, he gives *thanks to God*. After all, in his mind he is a *slave to* a *God's law*, though in his sinful nature "a slave to the law of sin".

2.F SLAVES, MORTAL BODIES, DEATH TO SIN (8:1-17)

Having more closely defined what it means to be a slave of righteousness (7:7-25 amplifying what we see in 6:15-23), Paul then shows that, because he is a slave to God's law in his mind, there is no condemnation to face. Note that he moves from first person to third person, then back to first person as he relates both his personal experience and that of all believers.

And the issue of law? He shows how he is a slave to righteousness, a slave to God's law in the mind, the victory being attained by the death of God's Son whose death enables us to see the righteous requirements of the law fulfilled in us, not merely through justification but through the sanctifying work of the Spirit, just as the following words disclose. In 6:1-14 Christ captures the spotlight, but here the Holy Spirit features prominently. Valuable instruction awaits those who reflect on why this is so.

Slaves, mortal bodies, death to sin

New life is now understood as living by the Spirit. The contrast now is not that between "the old self" and "the new life," but between those who live according to the sinful nature and those who live by the Spirit, who promises to give life to our mortal bodies as believers. We are to *put to death* the misdeeds of the body. Formerly it was stated we should no longer be slaves to sin; now we are reminded that in receiving the Holy Spirit we did not receive the cringing spirit of *a slave*.

2.E HOPE, GLORY, GOD'S LOVE IN CHRIST, THE HOLY SPIRIT (8:18-39)

Paul returns to the themes of hope in suffering, of glory, of the love of God, together with the consolation of the Holy Spirit.

He arrives at these themes after stressing the work of the Holy Spirit in the believer who is a child of God, an heir of God, a co-heir of Christ by first sharing in Christ's suffering before sharing in his glory.

What is new in the return to the aforementioned themes? Paul expands on what is exactly meant by the glory to come. Before he spoke of rejoicing in hope, now he speaks of groaning in hope. And he also speaks of groaning in hope before he proceeds to assure us we are beyond condemnation—as God is for us no matter what.

Hope, glory, God's love in Christ, the Holy Spirit

Our present *sufferings* cannot compare with the coming *glory*. In *hope* creation will be liberated. Just as suffering previously was viewed as good in that it erects the foundation for hope (see 5:3–5), so all things are now seen as working together for good in that God calls with a view to finally glorifying us. God *justifies*. No one can *condemn*.

2.D THE JEWS' ADVANTAGE, NO DIFFERENCE, CHILDREN OF PROMISE (9:1–11:36)

This is a lengthy part of the great inverted parallelism that can be said to form Romans, and the length of this part underlines the prominence Paul sought to give the issue of the status God's ancient people have in the light of the gospel.

It appears logical to believe Paul arrives quite naturally at the issue after stating nothing can separate us from the love of Christ (8:39). As he thinks of the impossibility of such a separation, he feels like wishing he could be cut off and thus separated from Christ for the sake of his ethnic people the Jews.

Previously Paul said the Jew was at an advantage—that there was even value in circumcision. Fleetingly he stated this before showing at greater length that Jews and Gentiles were alike in that they all have sinned. Now the apostle elaborates on the kind of advantage the Jew has (9:4–5). Some wonder if the Jews still have any advantage in the gospel after the apostle levels the field by stating there is no difference between Jew and Gentile in salvation as well as in sinning: "For there is no difference between Jew and Gentile—the same Lord is Lord of all and rightly blesses all who call on him . . ." (10:12).

Yet, to simply conclude there is no difference when it comes to salvation and leave it at that, fails to take into account the advantages Paul claims the Jews have. The apostle does not contradict himself, and thereupon shows that, while the Jewish nation is characterized by unbelief, the time is coming when the nation will be characterized by belief—not meaning a Jew can be saved without Christ, but that the nation will sometime in the future will be unlike it is now. All Israel will be saved, that is, in far greater numbers than at present.

The Jews' advantage, no difference, children of promise

The Jews are at *an advantage* (9:4–6) though it depends on—as it does for the Gentiles—on whom God has mercy for salvation. Abraham has children of promise. Believing that *Jesus rose from the dead* credits us with righteousness (4:24), which is tantamount to being saved (10:9). *There is no difference*—the same Lord blesses equally Jew and Gentile. *All* had sinned, but God will have mercy on *all*—that is, on both Jew and Gentile.

2.C DIVINE WRATH, BODY AND MIND, PASSING JUDGMENT (12:1–15:13)

David Seccombe is right in saying that, while the remainder of Romans is usually understood to be about "the Christian life," most of Romans deals with such a theme in its early references to faith, peace, walking in the Spirit, etc. Seccombe has the insight to recognize the uniqueness of Romans 12:1 on lies in the dealing with issues related to "practical Christian living in communities."[5]

Yet also to the point, Paul is drawing on the truth that, since God has shown mercy to us through his sovereign electing grace as Gentiles, and will do so on a greater scale in time to come for his ancient people, we are to worship God by conforming to his will "in view of [his] mercy." Much of the instruction from now to the end is put forward in the light of that mercy. Out of gratitude we are to do God's will.

Doing God's will because of the mercy showered on us is in direct contrast to life lived in defiance of God, a life of godlessness and wickedness as particularly portrayed in Romans 1 and 2. The contrast shows itself by the apostle causing the themes of wrath, body and mind, and the passing of judgment to reappear just before he closes the letter on a personal note that embraces greetings and benediction.

---

5. Seccombe, *Dust to Destiny* 204

2 Mirrors in Romans

Divine wrath, body and mind, passing judgment

Believers are urged to offer their *bodies* as living sacrifices to God, allowing their *minds* to be renewed.

Among other things, they are not to avenge themselves for any wrong done to them, but to leave room for God's *wrath*. Governing authorities are agents of God's present *wrath* to do good to believers. As sinners no one can pass judgment on another (2:1), and saints *passing judgment* on a fellow believer is also disallowed when it has to do with "disputable matters," matters of small account. Even believers will stand before God's *judgment seat* (compare 14:10 with what is said of unbelievers in 2:5).

True Jews by name are meant to give *praise to God* (recall 2:28), and in the believing community both Jew and Gentile are to live harmoniously, not engaging adversely in disputable matters between each other but accepting one other so as to *bring praise to God*. The believing Gentiles are particularly reminded to give *praise to God*.

2.B AMBITION, HINDRANCE, OBLIGATION (15:14-33)

Paul explains more fully why he had not come to the church in Rome earlier. Initially he merely said he had been prevented from coming. Now he explains he has been busy taking the gospel in Christ "from Jerusalem all the way around to Illyricum." When he says, "It has always been my ambition to preach the gospel," it sums up what he stated earlier: "I am obligated . . . " (1:14), "I am so eager . . . " (1:15), "I am not ashamed . . . ." (1:16).

Still, he longed to go to Rome after many years and he explains how it will come about.

Ambition, hindrance, obligation

Paul had been busy leading *Gentiles* to the gospel elsewhere, but now that there was no more room in the regions where he had been to preach the gospel to Gentiles, he hopes to have his *longing fulfilled* to see the Roman believers. He outlines his plan by which he hopes to see them. *Enjoying their company* (v.24) can be construed as including his desire to impart some spiritual gift to them (1:11). Running parallel with the constant object of taking the gospel to the Jew first (1:16) is *the debt Gentiles owe the Jews* in the way of spiritual blessings.

2. A PROPHECY, OBEDIENCE, BENEDICTION (16:1-27)

Paul ends his letter with personal greetings, as well as concluding with final advice or warning about divisions that may disrupt their obedience. Also he has benedictory words, and greetings as coming to the Roman church from others, finally ending the epistle with not a short benediction but one that is reminiscent of the opening of the epistle.

Prophecy, obedience, benediction

Peace was wished upon the believers right at the beginning, suggesting such peace would be granted in the present, but it seems the peace longed for in 16:20 has to do with the future when Christ thoroughly and ultimately crushes Satan, who is the instigator of the kind of discord Paul has warned the readers about. The *peace* will come soon in the sense that when it eventually comes, it will come quickly.

The *grace* spoken of is undoubtedly a present reality. What was viewed as *God's gospel* at the start is claimed by Paul to be his gospel as well. The gospel promised (1:2) is the gospel established. It has been promised beforehand but, until Christ came, it remained a mystery. Prophetic writings of old merely promised the gospel, but since the appearance of Christ it has been made known so *that all nations* might *believe* and *obey* God—this is the obedience that comes from faith that Paul wrote about in the beginning.

As God has revealed his wisdom in the gospel, all glory forever through Jesus Christ is to go to him.

3

Mirrors in Galations

WHILE AGREEING WITH MANY scholars about the outline of Galatians—that is to say, Paul's letter can be neatly divided for the large part into a doctrinal section and then into an ethical or moral section—it is also instructive to view Galatians in terms of steps that lead to a certain theological climax, which is then followed by Paul seeking to have his readers mirror in their lives what had been the apostle's experience.

The climax in Galatians comes in what has been commonly observed as the doctrinal argument. It is found in Galatians 3 and 4, where Paul theologically defends justification by faith. Before that, the apostle not only defends his own authority in preaching what he holds to be the gospel, but reveals autobiographically how he is convinced that Christl lives in him and he in Christ, having undergone crucifixion in order for him to live by faith in the Son of God. The doctrinal argument or rationale for such a conviction is buttressed by a well-reasoned view of what had been promised in Scripture before Christ came. Nevertheless, the doctrinal argument, as buttressed by conclusions drawn from Old Testament promises, and history and allegory, is reinforced through Paul's readers' own experience of what happened when they first believed. The doctrine of justification by faith could not be divorced from what Paul's readers had discovered upon them also believing, therefore to call Galatians 3 and 4 merely "doctrinal" can be misleading. Galatians 3 and 4 forms a climax not only because it focuses on the great doctrine of justification, but also on what the believers knew to be true upon reflection on what occurred when they first placed their faith in Christ as well.

In this letter a simple form of parallelism can be considered: A-B-C-D-D-C-B-A. It takes on board Galatians 3 and 4 as a climax of a kind, and so appears in the center of the chiasmus as "D." Catchwords and catchphrases link the three episodes on either side of "D," as will be shown below.

3. GALATIONS

Righteousness by faith in Christ

   A. Grace, peace, the world (1:1–5)

      B. No confusion must exist (1:6–24)

         C. Freedom, faith, circumcision, crucifixion (2:1–21)

            D. The Spirit, children of promise, bondage (3:1–4:31)

         C. Freedom, faith, circumcision, crucifixion (5:1–26)

      B. No confusion must exist (6:1–10)

   A. Grace, peace, the world (6:11–18)

3.A GRACE, PEACE, THE WORLD (1:1–5)

Paul's opening words hint at what will be the theme of the letter. Perhaps little will be found directly about Jesus' resurrection from death—there is more emphasis in the letter on the efficacy of his death—but the resurrection is often implied through the emphasis on the Holy Spirit, who has been sent into the hearts of believers as a result of Jesus' death. That Paul establishes he is an apostle of Christ as sent from God and not from or by man is to be noted—the establishment coming about through his own experience of personal revelation, which is in alignment with Old Testament prediction and the objective work of Christ in fulfilling such prediction.

The benediction is for the wish for grace and peace on Paul's readers, as well as stating Christ's purpose in giving himself for us.

Grace, peace, the world

The giving of himself (understood to be chiefly in dying on the cross) means Christ has rescued us from *the present evil age*. This enables believers to be recipients of *grace* and *peace*.

3.B NO CONFUSION MUST EXIST (1:6-24)

Paul is astonished that the newborn believers are quickly deserting the gospel, but hope for better things lies in exposing the perversity practiced by the false teachers who are responsible for any confusion. Paul is most dogmatic that eternal condemnation awaits anyone who persists in preaching a gospel different from what the believers had accepted as preached by Paul and his companions.

He is most dogmatic as born out of his personal experience of having had God reveal his son to him, on believing the gospel, after once holding doctrine quite similar to that practiced by the false teachers who were Judaizers as he had been. Why did Paul change so radically? By the grace of God that ran counter to his former Judaistic, legalistic way of life.

No confusion must exist

Some people sought to *confuse* the newborn believers with a perverted gospel. A perverted gospel if preached and practiced will lead to *eternal condemnation*.

3.C FREEDOM, FAITH, CIRCUMCISION, CRUCIFIXION (2:1-21)

On this side of the doctrinal section of the letter (Galatians 3 and 4) much of the stress is laid on Paul's horror at the quick desertion by the newborn believers, a horror based on what he personally had revealed to him (rather than discovered by him) of the true gospel, the gospel of grace. Note in Galatians 1 and 2 the common use of the first personal singular, as Paul traces how God revealed his son to him, how he was accepted by the apostolic leaders of Jerusalem who recognized him to be preaching the true gospel, how he faced Peter over the issue of Peter's hypocrisy in order to demonstrate no man—Jew or Gentile—is justified by the law, but only by faith in Christ.

Paul again draws on his personal experience in order to show it is not the law in terms of circumcision and the rest by which he lives—no, he has been crucified with Christ so that "I no longer live, but Christ lives in me".

It is a good question: If the law can justify, why did Christ die?

Freedom, faith, circumcision, crucifixion

Paul shows that the leaders of Jerusalem, though Jewish believers in Christ, did not require Gentile believers to be *circumcised*, thus leaving the Gentiles to enjoy the *freedom* there is in Christ.

Peter had feared the *circumcision* group at Antioch, but Paul exposed to Peter's face the hypocrisy of Jewish believers being seen to be superior to Gentile believers because the Gentiles were not circumcised.

The truth is no-one—Jew or Gentile—is justified by the law. The doctrine of the crucifixion of Christ is extended to mean Paul was also *crucified*, crucified with him in order to live by faith in the Son of God, who by inference is seen to be resurrected (recall the early comments on "Grace, Peace and the World").

Paul claims he personally has not set aside God's grace.

3.D THE SPIRIT, CHILDREN OF PROMISE, BONDAGE (3:1–4:31)

Paul leaves behind personal references to focus not on "I" but "you." This is before he launches into outlining the doctrine of justification by faith according to its historico-prophetic basis. Although he calls his readers "foolish," Paul patiently paints them into a corner to show that they have been bewitched. Note the new emphasis in terms of experience and the working of the Holy Spirit, as the Spirit's work was most manifest among the Galatians, so that on reflection they would see experientially the doctrine of justification by faith is true, as predicted years before Christ came.

The Galatians received *the Spirit* upon believing. The Spirit is spoken of in the context of the readers' believing in Christ's death for justification, as opposed to observing the law.

3 Mirrors in Galations

Paul's Gentile readers as believers are *children of Abraham*. Once again, the context is that of believing as opposed to observing the law. Scripture is employed by Paul to prove his thesis is correct.

History is called on to show the promise has to do with believing, so that the promise of becoming children of Abraham preceded the giving of the law, the law that held the whole world in bondage by making us *prisoners of sin*.

Paul reiterates what he said previously about the Gentiles being of Abraham's seed through faith in the gospel (3:26-29), but new in thought is the oneness that exists in Christ, irrespective of not just race but gender and social status.

While Paul drew attention to his readers' experience in the past upon receiving Christ in what has been traditionally viewed as the passage to do with the doctrinal meat of the letter, he now draws attention at quite some length to his readers' past *before* they came to faith in Christ (4:1-22). He reminds them of their past slavery to "the basic principles of the world." Had he wasted his efforts on them? Indeed, had they changed towards him, having become mesmerized by the false teachers?

As he seeks to rivet in his readers' minds that they are by faith in Christ children of promise, children of Abraham, children of "the free woman", an allegory is employed by the apostle, but it is based on truth that had already been established by him.

Simply called "the Spirit," or "*God's Spirit*" before in the letter, and with little qualification, the Spirit is viewed now as "*the Spirit of God's Son*", because the apostle is emphasizing that the believer's son-ship not only can be linked with Abraham and faith, but also with the reception of the Son's Spirit so that Abraham is not only the father of us—God himself is as well.

Before Christ' coming we were *prisoners* of the law, as well as *slaves* to the world's principles. *Imprisonment* and *slavery* are two ways of viewing bondage. This calls for some interesting reflection.

The *promise* had to do with an inheritance (3:18), and it has to do with freedom as well (4:21-31).

3.C FREEDOM, FAITH, CIRCUMCISION, CRUCIFIXION (5:1-26)

Paul pursues the theme of freedom from slavery after employing an allegory to highlight it. He is anxious that his readers do not devalue Christ by observing the law and falling thus from grace. "Faith expressing itself through love" is what counts.

Agitators are at work to undermine the readers' trust in Christ, and an antidote for this is to serve one another in the counter-community of faith, serving one another in love.

The community of faith will fulfil the very law its opponents stress—agitators know nothing of the unity of the law through love. Unity lies in love, not legalism. Moreover, the freedom to love could be achieved by the brothers because of the indwelling Holy Spirit. Crucifixion of the believers' sinful nature has taken place by belonging to Christ, and it is by keeping in step with the Spirit that the overcoming of any acts of the sinful nature can now be accomplished.

Freedom, faith, circumcision, crucifixion

Previously the apostle referred to opponents spying out "*the freedom we have in Christ.*" He was referring to his and Titus' freedom, but now he speaks of the freedom of his readers being threatened in Galatia (cf. 2:4 and 5:1).

Paul still sounds out about *circumcision* and its threat to *freedom* in the light of being *justified*, still viewing faith as that which alone justifies, only here he couples faith with love (v.6), "love" becoming a key word when he calls on the Galatians to love one another and think in terms of living in the Spirit because crucifixion has taken place in them. Previously Paul wrote of being *crucified* with Christ and living by faith in the Son of God (2:20), but now he spells it out for his readers as *crucifixion* of their sinful nature, together with the need to live by the Spirit. The issue previously was more to do with justification through Christ alone, whereas in exhorting the believers to exercise faith through love he speaks of them being already justified and calls on them to go forward in living by the Spirit, being led by the Spirit, and keeping in step with the Spirit. This is living after the sinful nature had been slain.

3.B NO CONFUSION TO EXIST (6:1–10)

Catchphrase-wise, catchword-wise, there is no connection between 6:1–10 and 1:6–23. Any similarity that lies between the two passages stems from the warnings Paul issues to the readers about deserting the gospel or being deceived within themselves so that they are found mocking God. We need to be clear-headed about what is the true gospel, and we need to be clear-headed so as not to deceive ourselves into thinking we are "something" when we are "nothing" (6:3).

When we are clear about what constitutes the true gospel and are not confused (1:6–9), we may seek to restore others who are confused but do so without a sinful sense of superiority. This is what Paul speaks about in 6:1–10. It is only natural that he included a word of caution for the more enlightened who think they are "something" because they are more enlightened. Intellectually they may be, but they need to be "spiritual" in order to restore brothers caught in sin.

Being "spiritual" had already been defined (5:13–26) and, while the sin that one may be caught in and be overtaken by is not defined, it would include being caught off guard by the kind of perversion of the gospel that he warns about, with all the bad effects Paul also warns about.

No confusion to exist

One may *desert* God through being manipulated by false teachers who pervert the gospel, (1:6), and one may be *deceived* within by being proud in comparing himself with others. No one can desert God without serious consequences. No-one can turn their nose up at God in pride without serious consequences. To desert God means *eternal condemnation*. To mock him means reaping *destruction* (6:7).

3.A GRACE, PEACE, THE WORLD (6:11–18)

As Paul closes his letter to the Galatians, he speaks of the boasting the false teachers will make by triumphing over the brothers in getting them circumcised, and then makes plain he boasts only in the cross of Christ, whereby the world is crucified to Paul and he to the world. Peace and mercy is sought for all believers, and included is the hope for many who prove to be faithful believers among the Jews as well. Divine grace is sought for the readers' spirits.

Grace, peace, the world

At the beginning of the letter Christ is said to have given himself up for believers' sins; at the letter's end such divine rescue is simplified in definition by the term *"the cross."* And what was originally described as *"the present evil age"* is simplified in definition by the term *"the world."* For Paul, being rescued by Christ, who gave himself for our sins, is synonymous with being crucified to the world and the world to him. The object in rescuing us lay not only in Christ giving himself up for our sins, but in our own crucifixion.

Because it is a present evil age, the world must be dealt "a death blow,"[1] just as the world dealt Paul one. His allusion to this by reference to bearing in his body the marks of Jesus bears witness to it.

Grace and *peace* come to be more replete in meaning in the close of the letter than in its opening words.

---

1. Guthrie

4

Mirrors in Ephesians

MODERN SCHOLARS BY AND large have concluded that Ephesians was more than likely a circular letter to a number of churches, hence the lack of personal greetings at the beginning and the end of the letter. Several important witnesses in early days did not include the words "in Ephesus," though Ephesus might have been the main church to which copies of the letter were sent.[1]

The contents of the letter argue well for it being a circular epistle. It refers to no particular problems (as we find in what many have called a sister letter to Colossae). It is the only Pauline letter that does not address particular problems of the church or churches to which it is directed. Besides Paul, Tychicus is the only other person referred to, but he is merely mentioned at the end of the letter as one who was to be the courier of the letter and the envoy to the churches of the province of Asia that had been planted during Paul's Ephesian ministry.[2] It was a letter that could well serve as a general one since its theme is God's purpose for the whole church. Only 1 Corinthians outranks Ephesians in the use of the word "church," but the contents of Ephesians portray a greater overview of what the church is and is destined to be, irrespective of where any local congregation is situated.

The great letter begins and virtually ends on the theme of the "heavenly realms." The beginning of the letter truly reflects what its contents will be. The church on earth may seem to be a far cry from what Paul imagines is its potential power when considering the promised blessing as coming from

1. Metzer, *A Textual Commentary*, 532
2. F.F. Bruce, *The Epistle to the Ephesians*, 135

the heavenly realms, but Paul reveals how the blessing of God in believers on earth is a blessing in tune with such potential. In the heavenly realms God chose his children on earth long before they believed, with rich grace that enables them to discern God's disclosed will, which is to bring all things ultimately together both in heaven and earth under one head, even Christ.

Paul then shows that in this time of interregnum, the government of Christ in the church at least, is not entirely suspended but is well exercised now in order that the body of Christ will grow towards full stature as the church, though it amounts to no small struggle, as believers are besought to grow up corporately in Christ and to take account of the evil spiritual forces in the heavenly realms.

F.F. Bruce says "some allusions to foregoing themes" are to be discerned in Ephesians 6:10–20, but he does not draw direct attention to its connection to 1:3–10, even though in his admirable step-by-step outline of Ephesians he refers at the beginning to the theme of praising God for his great blessings in the heavenly realms, and ends by referring to the major spiritual battle being engaged in the heavenly realms.

Of course, an admirable step-by-step reading of Ephesians has precedence in the way we approach Ephesians—development of thought is most crucial for our understanding—but it is also useful, if a chiastic form is discerned, to deepen our understanding through comparisons and contrasts within the letter.

Such can be achieved in Ephesians, even though the chiastic structure is a little more intricate than in some other writings. A suggested structure is: A-B-W-X-Y-Z-W-X-Y-Z-B-A. The letter begins and ends on the note of grace and peace. Moving in, the theme of "the heavenly realms" is detected (B). Then follows the step-by-step movement through themes twice covered: Gentiles (W) —prayer for the fullness of God (X) —good works (Y) —one body (Z) —Gentiles (W) —prayer for the fullness of God (X) —good works (Y) —one body (Z).

4 Mirrors in Ephesians

4. EPHESIANS

God's Plan For the Church

   A. Grace and peace (1:1–2)

      B. The heavenly realms (1:3–10)

           W. Inclusive salvation (1:11–14)

              X. Prayer for power (1:15–23)

                 Y. Good works (2:1–10)

                    Z. One body (2:11–22)

           W. Inclusive salvation (3:1–13)

              X. Prayer for power (3:14–21)

                 Y. Good works (4: 1–16)

                    Z. One body (4:17–6:9)

      B. The heavenly realms (6:10–20)

   A. Grace and peace (6:21–24)

4.A GRACE AND PEACE (1:1–2)

The greeting is quite simple after Paul introduces himself.

Grace and peace

Paul as the apostolic author of the letter wishes not only *peace* for the believers but God's *unearnt favor* (grace).

4.B THE HEAVENLY REALMS (1:3–10)

In one grand long, long sentence—in fact, it can be viewed as extending from v. 3 to v. 14 in 202 words [3]—Paul pours forth phrase upon phrase in praise of a gathering momentum when contemplating God's eternal

---

3. Hendriksen, *Ephesians* (Banner of Truth), 72

purpose to culminate his sovereignty in bringing all things under one head through Christ, in whom we who believe (both Jew and Gentile) have been chosen to "the praise of his glory."

Praise begins with contemplation of the heavenly realms (where we are blessed), then focuses on the earth in contemplation of Christ's redemption of us, up to that of the coming reconciliation of both heaven and earth, then down to earth again as our thoughts are taken up with Jew and Gentile being chosen to believe.

Moving nearer to the end of his praise, Paul's thanks reaches the penultimate: spelling out the blessings of the heavenly realms being presently experienced through Christ's redemptive power on earth before he declares God's purpose of reconciling heaven and earth under Christ's headship.

The heavenly realms

We are blessed in Christ with *every spiritual blessing in the heavenly realms*. The heavenly places are viewed as under God the Father's sovereign power, he exercising his will freely and according to his holy pleasure. His will is such that nothing will prevent Christ from becoming head in heaven and earth ultimately.

4.W INCLUSIVE SALVATION (1:11-14)

God's plan for Christ's ultimate headship embraces both believing Jew and Gentile. It becomes apparent that by stating "we were also chosen," Paul refers to believing Jews, describing himself and his fellow believing countrymen as "the first to hope in Christ." By declaring "*you* also were included in Christ" he is referring to Gentiles. In the early days it was the Gentiles who had to be assured that they were in Christ and were inheritors as well of the coming glory.

Inclusive salvation

In Christ *Paul and other believing Jews* were chosen. *The Gentiles* ("you also") were included to share hope in Christ as well. They too will share in God's *inheritance*.

4.X PRAYER FOR POWER (1:15-23)

Having established that both Jew and Gentile are chosen of God, and will both share in the future inheritance, Paul has cleared the way to show his prayer is intended "for all the saints", that is, Jew and Gentile.

This prayer, like the foregoing praise of God the Father, comprises a long, long sentence. In the original it is a single sentence of 169 words.[4] Both in praise of the Father and prayer for the saints, Paul can barely contain himself. It is good to translate as the original has it in order to go, as it were, with Paul, up the spiral staircase from being thankful for the saints' love and faith, to asking the Father to give the knowledge they need to possess hope and riches and power, which power is not merely a power "toward us" but one that has enabled Christ to rise to an unparalleled height over all things.

How does such power of Christ dovetail in what was earlier said about him having all things united in him, in the future things in heaven and on earth? It is in the fullness of time that such power over all things will be exercised. In the present Christ exercises unlimited power for the sake of the church, his body, as he must—otherwise the church could not have come into being and continue to exist until the fullness of time.

Prayer for power

Because God, according to his eternal plan, has done so much to give his saints a foretaste through the Holy Spirit of the inheritance to come, Paul is inspired to give thanks, and then to pray that the saints' eyes will be opened more to what is to come and to Christ's present power for his body, the church. Thus Paul says "For this reason . . . " He speaks of *prayers*, so that one may safely conclude that Paul regularly gave thanks and regularly prayed for the kind of things he states in the letter.

He addresses God as *the Father of glory*, praying the saints will know the greatness of God's immeasurable *power* towards *we who believe*.

In prayer he also contemplates both *this age* and the one to come.

The church is viewed as Christ's body.

---

4. Hendriksen Ephesians, (Banner of Truth) 95

4.Y GOOD WORKS (2:1-10)

Since Paul does not qualify "you" in 2.1—as he does in 2:11—we may safely presume Paul reminds Jew and Gentile that once they were both dead in trespasses and sins. He describes the saints in their former unbelief in various ways, but he chiefly has deadness in trespasses and sins in mind, as he moves on to speak at some length about the saints being raised while dead—to sit in the heavenly places in Christ. He does this to highlight the immeasurable riches of God's grace to come, as well as his present grace, in order that the saints—out of gratitude for what is to come and what they presently know as grace—will be provoked into seeing that they have been created in Christ for good works.

Good works

Paul says we are God's workmanship, created in Christ for *good works*, which God *prepared beforehand* that we should walk in them. Once the saints walked the way of trespasses and sins (2:1), now they are to walk in what they have been created for in Christ.

4.Z ONE BODY (2:11-22)

Gentiles are to be especially grateful for salvation, as once they were separated from Christ, and alienated from the commonwealth of Israel, strangers to the covenants of promise, having no hope, and without God in the world. Now they have been brought near through Christ's blood. Christ has broken down the barrier between Gentile and Jew. Gentile and Jew are now one body, the Gentile joining the Jew to become one body. (Note it is not the Jew joining the Gentile, but the other way around.)

Now it is in Christ they are one body, with Jew and Gentile sharing equal privileges in becoming fellow citizens in the building of the household of God. Together in Christ they become the structure of God's temple.

One body

Through Christ's blood the barrier between Jew and Gentile is broken down. The wall has been pulled down and Gentiles are coming into the commonwealth of Israel to be *one body* with them.

4.W INCLUSIVE SALVATION (3:1-13)

In the early stages of the church's history the Gentiles had to be made welcome, since it appeared that Christ came only for Israel. The Gentiles had to feel that they could believe in Christ as well, when it appeared they were not full citizens or on equal standing with Jews in Christ. It is plain Paul goes to considerable lengths to assure believing Gentiles they are on equal standing with believing Jews, even though the commonwealth is of Israel (2:12).

Paul's prayer begins but is left suspended when in a lengthy parenthesis he seeks to explain that he is imprisoned because he had been taking the gospel particularly to Gentiles so that unbelieving Jews took offence and had him incarcerated.

Here is a defense of Paul's ministry to the Gentiles. There were hints in the Old Testament revelation that God would embrace Gentiles in the plan of salvation, but it needed clear revelation upon the coming of Christ. Paul received a special revelation to that effect, so too did Christ's "holy apostles and prophets by the Spirit." It was revealed that the Gentiles would be "fellow heirs," "members of the same body [of the Jews]." Paul, out of undeserving grace, became an apostle to the Gentiles so as to bring to light God's plan for the church of Jew and Gentile, therefore he and his Gentile readers could afford to be bold in Christ and not lose heart.

Inclusive salvation

Paul was a prisoner for *the Gentiles*. *Gentiles* share equal standing with Jews in Christ. Paul was commissioned to minister to *Gentiles* because God's plan embraced them. Therefore *the Gentiles* were not to lose heart because Paul was suffering for their cause.

4.X PRAYER FOR POWER (3:14-21)

This completes the prayer Paul began before he digressed to explain to his Gentile believers why they did not need to be ashamed of him being a prisoner for preaching to Gentiles.

It is most edifying to compare this prayer with that found in 1:15-23. Like that prayer, it addresses the Gentile as well as Jewish believers, though the earlier petition appeals to them both on a more individual level.

Mirrors in Mark (and in other New Testament Writings)

Little work has been done by scholars to compare the two prayers, and it is not within the scope of this book to compare them at length. However, it is interesting that one scholar[5] proposed that the link between the two prayers lies in the first prayer being an entreaty for "the impartation of heavenly wisdom", and the second one brings the entreaty of the first to "its conclusion." Unfortunately, he does not elaborate.

It could be claimed that the earlier prayer for the impartation of heavenly wisdom is concluded in 3:14–21, if we keep in mind that Paul's thought in this letter is propelling itself towards the notion of the oneness that ought to exist between Jew and Gentile. That oneness is not really apparent in the first part of the prayer—if we view both prayers as forming a whole and having a climax in the second prayer or part—but becomes so in the conclusion of 3:14–21. Prior to praying for the second time as it were, Paul had been working towards establishing in the hearts of the believers the doctrine of one body in Christ, which is the burden of the letter.

A key expression in 3:14–21 is "together with all saints," falling in line with the apostle's words of 2:11–22, where the theme is "one in Christ."

Similar expressions in both parts of the prayer show the link between the two.

Prayer for power

"For this reason," says Paul, "I kneel before the Father." The desire is that God out of his *riches* will strengthen the believers through Christ dwelling in their hearts *with power*. The *fullness* of God is the ultimate in knowledge. *Power* that is for us (1:19) is also power within us. God is to be glorified in *the church* and in Christ. God's power is both incomparable (1:19) and immeasurable (3:20).

4.Y GOOD WORKS (4:1–16)

Previously Paul spoke of the believers being created for good works (2:10). Now he reveals by what vehicle the good works will be performed. Keeping the believers as a whole in mind, he shows how that oneness in Christ is to be attained (4:1–6). He reveals that while oneness is to be striven for, particular persons have unique gifts in order "to prepare God's people for

---

5. F.F. Bruce, *The Epistle to the Ephesians*

works of service," that is, for good works. Christ in his ascending power has set apart certain persons to prepare God's people for works in order that "the body of Christ may be built up." Gifted men do not threaten the oneness but are enabled to achieve it. And good works help cement the oneness that is to be achieved.

The unity of the Spirit can be accomplished when believers "make every effort" to keep it (4:3), but such a unity is to be identified with reaching it by faith and knowledge in the Son of God so that maturity is found in the whole measure of fullness of Christ being realized. In context "the unity of the faith and knowledge of the Son of God" is more closely identified with the role of the gifted ones of the community than with the previously mentioned unity of the Spirit, as it is the gifted people who prepare believers through such divine knowledge for "works of service."

Good works

In what mirrors 2:1–10, *the ascension of Christ* is to be noted once more. Previously Christ's ascension was seen in terms of believers being raised with him. Now his ascension is linked with a victory that enables him to shower gifts on men. Those who are given gifts are given them to prepare God's people for *works of service*.

4.Z ONE BODY (4:17–6:9)

In mirroring 2:11–22, this large part is taken up with the desired solidarity that should exist between all believers as they do the good works gifted men prepare them for.

Paul speaks of being one body in the new context of Christ having broken down the barrier between Jew and Gentile (2:11–22), and prays that together with all the saints the fullness of God may be known (3:14–21), ethically through the unity of the Spirit (4:1–6), humbly by acknowledging those who are gifted to prepare them for good works (4:7–16). In the togetherness of love and through the truth that binds believers, they form the body of Christ as "each part does its work" (4:16).

As each part does its work, all the admonitions covered by 4:17 to 6:9 will be heeded and thus the whole body of Christ will function as it should. Some relationships are more personal or particular—such as between husband and wife—but they also contribute to the body of Christ by being held together. A ruptured relationship between a believing husband and wife affects the holding together of Christ's body more than many perhaps realize.

One body

While Paul appeals to us individually in his admonitions to do good works, in his spelling out of what good works consist of, there is considerable stress on us as the body of Christ, and consequently he stresses the social implications there are in practicing the works that he outlines.

In putting off our old self we are to speak truthfully to our neighbor (fellow-believer), "for we are members of *one body*" (v.25).

Among other things, we are to speak to one another through music, and submit to each other generally and in more personal relationships.

4.B THE HEAVENLY REALMS (6:10-20)

The Father might have blessed us in the heavenly realms, and Christ is to bring all things in heaven and on earth together under his headship ultimately, but we must be on guard, since in the same heavenly realms where we are said to be blessed there are great forces of evil endeavoring to bring us down on an evil day. All believers are to be alert to those days or times that will be particularly testing. The only way to combat the evil spirits in the heavenly realms is by putting on God's armor. As believers we must be on guard against being presumptuous, yes, even though we have been chosen of God for salvation.

The instructions concerning the armor of God in 6:10-20 serve as a sound counter-balance to the blessings enumerated in 1:3-10.

The heavenly realms

We are to make ourselves strong in the Lord with the armor of God, so as to war against the powers that wreak havoc in this dark world and whose origins are of *the heavenly realms*. We who believe are blessed in the heavenly realms for God has made known to us the mystery of his will (connect with 1:9). Paul requests prayer (as prayer is part of the warfare against the hostile unseen forces) so that he can declare *the mystery* of the gospel (6:19).

4.A GRACE AND PEACE (6:21-24)

Tychicus is to be sent so that the churches may be encouraged by news of Paul. A benediction closes the circular letter in a somewhat similar way to the benediction opening it.

Grace and peace

Peace is prayed for, except that in these final words it is coupled with faith and love. *Grace* is coupled with love too, being wished for those who love the Lord Jesus Christ with undying love.

5

Mirrors in Philippians

When mirroring is considered in any biblical composition, it needs to be said that (to change the metaphor) wherever there is development of thought there may well be a bridge to span what is common ground. This we have seen in Romans and the passage found there in 7:1-6, which is a small but important bridge. The common ground, which can be close because of the shortness of the bridge, ought to be noticed quite readily, but it may not be seen. A case in point is the common ground of Philippians 2:1–11 and 2:19–30.

The theme or common ground in mind has to do with "the interest of others," in the first instance as related to Christ's example, in the second as connected with Timothy's and Epaphroditus' examples. Not all scholars have picked up on it.

Timothy and Epaphroditus' selflessness served as proof that Christ's example could be imitated.[1] Not only was Timothy's particular help crucial, and proof positive that Christ's example could be copied, but his Christ-like character was to be formative in boosting the believers' confidence through hearing of Paul's news and in carrying back news of them to Paul as well.

Several outlines of Philippians by a few scholars show they have at least seen some *comparison* in 2:1–11 and 2:19–30. William McDonald puts one heading after another to show his awareness of the link by way of comparison: "Exhortation to unity based on Christ's example of humiliation" and "The Christlike example of Paul, Timothy and Epaphroditus."[2]

1. *Calvin's Commentaries*, Vol. XXI, 21 (Baker Book House)
2. McDonald, *Believer's Bible Commentary*,

5 Mirrors in Philippians

Sinclair Ferguson differs a little from McDonald by detaching 2:12–18 from 2:1–11, and then gives two titles to 2:19–30. Still, he sees the mirror of Christ's example in the example of Timothy and Epaphroditus.[3] He calls Paul's references to the two servants of Christ of Timothy and Epaphroditus in their imitation of Christ "gentle hints" to the Philippians that they ought in imitation to follow those two men's examples. It is interesting to pursue a study by way of *contrast* between Christ and the two Christ-like men.

Now, in terms of comparisons and contrasts there are even more than those in 2:1–11 and 2:19–30.

5. PHILIPPIANS

Joy in the Lord

  A. Greetings to all the saints (1:1–2)

    B. Partnership and fruit (1:3–11)

      C. Defense of the gospel and rejoicing (1:12–18a)

        D. Gaining in Christ and standing firm (1:18b–30)

          E. Interest in others (2:1–11)

            F. Working out salvation (2:12–18)

          E. Interest in others (2:19–30)

        D. Gaining in Christ and standing firm (3:1–4:1)

      C. Defense of the gospel and rejoicing (4:2–9)

    B. Partnership and fruit (4:10–20)

  A. Greetings to all the saints (4:21–23)

5.A GREETINGS TO ALL THE SAINTS (1:1–2)

"To all the saints" is an expression peculiar to Philippians and among the Pauline letters. It is found at both the beginning and the end of the letter. The word "all" frequently occurs in a letter that has little to say by the way of rebuke to any of the saints. Paul possessed warm feelings towards Philippi

---

3. *Let's Study Philippians*, XVII (Banner of Truth)

as a church, for it stood out in practical support of the apostle. Even those rebuked (4:2,3) are still admired for the support of Paul and the gospel in the past, so that the word "all" when applied to the Philippian saints glows in appreciation of them as a whole.

Greetings to all the saints

To all the saints, together with the overseers and deacons, goes out the benediction of grace and peace.

5.B PARTNERSHIP AND FRUIT (1:3-11)

Partnership in the gospel has meant the church at Philippi inspires Paul to render thanks to God, and finds Paul confident that Christ will complete the good work he began in them. He prays with thanks, and he prays the saints will become even more fruitful.

Partnership and fruit

From *the first day* the Philippians' *partnership* in the gospel was evident. Paul in prayer thanks God with joy for this. Yet, also in prayer, he longs that the good work Christ began in them would be completed. How would it be completed? By their love abounding, by their discernment being heightened with the object of them being filled with the *fruit* of righteousness so as to be blameless when Christ returns.

5.C DEFENSE OF THE GOSPEL AND REJOICING (1:12-18A)

One can see on becoming familiar with Philippians that defense and confirmation of the gospel was much on the apostle's mind as he wrote to Philippi (1:7), and how those saints endeared themselves to Paul by being partners in that gospel. Could there be a defense or confirmation of the gospel if Paul was in chains (see 1:7 again)? Yes, there was in leading others to evangelize.

Defense of the gospel and rejoicing

The gospel was advanced though Paul was in chains. Most brothers in the Lord were encouraged to become bolder in their witness. Even where there was ill-feeling towards Paul, there was still *a defense of the gospel* on the part of those who wished to stir up further trouble for the imprisoned Paul. No matter what motive drove some to advance the gospel, it was being preached, and that led Paul to *rejoice*.

5.D GAINING IN CHRIST AND STANDING FIRM (1:18B–30)

Although Paul was in chains, and although he cared not if he lived or died (either way he belonged to Christ), he was quite convinced he would survive his imprisonment, as it appeared he would not die but live for the Philippians' progress and joy in the faith. Yet, whatever happened to him, Paul's desire was for the Philippians to stay firm in the faith and suffer for Christ.

Gaining in Christ and standing firm

If Paul were to die it would be *gain*, since there would be no loss when it was better to be with Christ. Amid enemies and those who *opposed* them, the call to the saints is to *stand firm* and *suffer* for Christ. Their enemies' destiny is *destruction*.

5.E INTEREST IN OTHERS (2:1–11)

To stand firm in the faith it was essential for the saints to be united, to have "the same love," to be "one in spirit and in purpose." This would be achieved by being humble and looking out for the interest of others, as well as their own. Christ is portrayed by Paul as looking out for our interest, despite by nature being God. We should have the same attitude as Christ.

Interest in others (2:1–11)

On account of the experience we have in being united with Christ and all that it means (2:1), we ought to be united in humility, looking out *for the interest of others*. We should emulate our now exalted Christ in what had been his once humbled state.

5.F WORKING OUT SALVATION (2:12-17)

Before going on to show how Timothy and Epaphroditus are Christ-like examples, Paul fixes attention at the midpoint of his letter on how the saints at Philippi ought to conduct themselves in his absence. Without Paul, they are to continue to work out their own salvation (not depending on the hope of the apostle's presence). On one hand, they are to work out inwardly their salvation with fear and trembling. On the other, they are to shine outwardly as stars while they hold out or hold on to the word of life for. Even if Paul is to die, they should rejoice at the prospect of what will be on the day of Christ.

5.E INTEREST IN OTHERS (2:19-30)

Under the Roman Emperor Nero, Paul hoped for a favorable verdict in the imperial court, but he could not be absolutely sure if he would be favored with release and so avoid death. He may make complete before God what sacrifice the Philippians by their life of faith had offered by an accompanying offering of his own death. This should cause rejoicing, both on the apostle's part and that of the Philippians. His death would endorse their own sacrificial faith.

Yet Paul would also be heartened if Timothy were to go soon to Philippi and then return with news of the believers. Meanwhile Epaphroditus would be sent with news from Paul.

Interest in others

Paul was most eager to send Timothy to the believers, as Timothy epitomized all that the believers should be in imitation of Christ (2:1–5). Says Paul: "(Timothy) takes *a genuine interest in your welfare. For everyone looks out for his own interests, not those of Jesus Christ.*"

Epaphroditus would be first sent to Philippi, as one who also bore similarity to Christ, being described as *"risking his life to make up for the help you could not give me."*

5.D GAINING IN CHRIST AND STANDING FIRM (3:1–4:1)

This forms a considerable bulk of Paul's letter, as he bids the Philippians once more to not only rejoice but also reflect again on what Paul sees as loss for the gain of Christ (see 1:21). It is viewing loss and gain from another angle, and it helps to reinforce Paul's admonition for all the believers to stand firm amid enemies of the gospel.

Gaining in Christ and standing firm

The brothers are to *rejoice*. They are to be wary of those whose sole concern is for lesser things in terms of worshipping God. Those lesser things once occupied the apostle's mind in his misplaced zeal for God, but such things are regarded as "loss for the sake of Christ." His goal is to *gain Christ* through divine righteousness and a personal knowledge of him.

Paul presses on to perfection in Christ, inspiring his readers to follow his example, while they remain wary of the gospel's opponents (cf. 3:18 and 19, 2:28), whose destiny is *destruction*.

He has shown how they should *stand firm*.

5.C DEFENSE OF THE GOSPEL AND REJOICING (4:2–9)

Previously Paul had shown himself tolerant to a degree of those who preached Christ from dubious motives but, where there was such disagreement between those who had assisted Paul in the preaching of the gospel, he is anxious for them to dissolve their disagreement in order that the course of the gospel is not hindered.

Once more, the apostle bids his readers to rejoice. There is every reason to rejoice in the light of his following words about the things that make for peace with God (vv.5–9a). For twice he speaks by a form of conclusion about the peace of God.

Defense of the gospel and rejoicing

Paul bids two women of the church to agree with each other, for it is tragic in the light of them having *contended at Paul's side for the cause of the gospel*. Twice he bids all believers to rejoice, and twice speaks of the peace of God in instructions that follow.

5.B PARTNERSHIP AND FRUIT (4:10-20)

Paul returns to the theme of partnership and fruit. A more literal translation than the NIV makes the parallel with 1:3-11 more patent.

Earlier on, the apostle made mention of partnership in the gospel, which partnership—while not closely defined—in all likelihood consisted of co-operating with Paul in gospel witness.[4] It was a partnership from the first day Paul visited the believers' city. Such a recollection endeared Paul to them so he fervently prayed that in light of the coming Day of Christ they may be filled with the fruit of righteousness.

Towards the close of the letter the apostle now speaks of partnership through the believers giving him gifts in support of his gospel work. This is present fruit for the believers, as part of further fruitfulness to come when Paul's prayer of 1:9-11 is answered to the full.

Partnership and fruit

No church had entered into *partnership* with Paul through the giving of gifts as Philippi had done.

Their gifts had Paul seeking *the fruit* that would increase to their credit (see ESV for v.17). "Gifts" and "fruit" are the kind of thing Ronald A. Ward calls "near neighbors," unlikely words brought together.[5] It would seem more natural to think of the apostle getting the fruit of the Philippians' labors through their gifts, but the gifts for Paul bring forth fruit to the givers! If we hark back to 1:9-11, we are to recognize it as the fruit of righteousness for them.

5.A GREETINGS TO ALL THE SAINTS (4:21-23)

In closing the letter, "all the saints" appears twice as an expression.

Greetings to all the saints

All the saints are greeted, and *all the saints* with Paul send their greetings as well.

---

4. F.F. Bruce *Philippians* (New International Biblical Commentary)
5. 'Ronald A. Ward, *Hidden Meaning In the New Testament,* (Marshall, Morgan & Scott)

6
Mirrors in 1 Timothy

BECAUSE 1 TIMOTHY COVERS a wide range of matters such as personal advice to Timothy, church government and order, an attempt to find chiastic order is more difficult, and when found it shows itself as more complex. Some attempts to find chiasmi can make a laughing stock of this type of structure. Some have claimed to have discovered chiasmi that actually prove to be far too complex to aid the memory.

A useful guide to aid memorization of 1 Timothy is naturally more complex than that found so far in this work (more complex than Ephesians, for instance). Of the shorter New Testament works, 1 Timothy is most intricate. All the same, for a trained mind the chiastic structure is not too taxing to take on board. Four balancing chiasmi—leaving aside the greeting and the benediction at the beginning and end of the letter—can be discerned, and of the following order:

A B C B A (1:3–20)

D E F G F E D (2:1–3:16)

H I J I H (4:1–5:16)

K L M N M L K (5:17–6:21a)

6. 1 TIMOTHY

Instructions for governing the church

Greeting and grace (1:1–2)

Mirrors in Mark (and in other New Testament Writings)

   A. Good conscience (1:3–7)
      B. The glorious gospel and God's glory (1:8–11)
         C. The merciful God (1:12–14)
      B. The glorious gospel and God's glory (1:15–17)
   A. Good conscience (1:18–20)

    D. Testimony of the truth (2:1–7)
      E. A word to men (2:8)
        F. A word to women (2:9–15)
          G. Church leaders (3:1–10)
        F. A word to women (3:11)
      E. A word to men (3:12–13)
    D. Testimony of the truth (3:14–16)

     H. Abusing the faith, and marriage (4:1–5)
       I. Training and progress (4:6–8)
         J. A saying of full acceptance (4:9–10)
       I. Training and progress (4:11–16)
     H. Abusing the faith, and marriage (5:1–16)

       K. Honoring divine trust (5:17–23)
         L. Good deeds (5:24–25)
           M. Respect for our superior (6:1–2)
             N. Wealth and godliness (6:3–10)
           M. Respect for our superior (6:11–16)
         L. Good deeds (6:17–19)
       K. Honoring divine trust (6:20–21a)

6 Mirrors in 1 Timothy

Benediction and grace (6:21b)

Greeting and Grace (1:1–2)

Addressing Timothy, among other things Paul prays that grace will be his.

1 Timothy 1:3–20

   A. Good conscience (1:3–7)

      B. The glorious gospel and God's glory (1:8–11)

         C. The merciful God (1:12–14)

      B. The glorious gospel and God's glory (1:15–17)

   A. Good conscience (1:18–20)

6A. GOOD CONSCIENCE (1:3–7)

Certain men were to be reined in by Timothy because they taught false doctrine. Paul states then what true doctrine is. Paul has in mind some who were wandering from what constitutes true doctrine, therefore such men are to be viewed not as infiltrators of the church but as belonging to the community of faith. Even believers may be teachers of the law, as if we can legislate men into the kingdom in a kind of restoration theology, which is a far cry from making known the gospel that alone saves. *Some have wandered away* from true doctrine and from what essentially saves. They are not holding on to love, *faith* and *a good conscience*.

6.B THE GLORIOUS GOSPEL AND GOD'S GLORY (1:8–11)

The law was designed only for public lawbreakers, whereas the gospel possesses sound and saving doctrine in conformation with the blessedness or the absolute perfection and completeness of God.[1] The law was designed to curb sin, particularly of a public nature; it could not save. The gospel does save as a positive force, and as an exhibition of the glory of *the blessed God*.

---

1. Hendriksen, *Timothy and Titus* (Banner of Truth), 71

6.C THE MERCIFUL GOD (1:12-14)

The words of Paul here form the centerpiece of the first chiasmus. It is pivotal, since it enlightens us as to how Paul came to be a servant of God. It came about through the very gospel he has already promoted and portrayed as fitting in with the blessedness and perfection of God. He infers the law (see vv.8-11 again) was impotent to bring about the faith and love required in Christ Jesus.

6.B THE GLORIOUS GOSPEL AND GOD'S GLORY (1:15-17)

Although there are no key words or phrases completely identical to those of 1:8-11, certain expressions of 1:15-17 are synonymous with some found in that earlier passage. The mirroring is here as Paul continues to give personal testimony to the grace of God. The law does not save sinners. Moreover, unlike the law, the gospel glorifies God, says Paul in reiteration of what he states in 1:8-11. The theme is the same but new light illuminates our understanding even more. Christ came to *save sinners* (so meets sound doctrine) and it is such a salvation that redounds to the glory of God, which lies and lives in him as *the King eternal, immortal, invisible, the only God.*

6.A A GOOD CONSCIENCE (1:18-20)

Paul reiterates what he said previously about some men erring. What is new in thought is the instruction of a more personal kind to hold onto faith and a good conscience, viewing it as a fight to do so- making it a good fight. It is stated against the grim news that some are not following such a course. God desires people to come to the knowledge of *the truth*. The truth lies in Christ's ransoming power. *The testimony* of it found Paul being a herald and an apostle to proclaim it. Timothy is instructed to hold on to *faith* and *a good conscience*, knowing "some have rejected these and so have shipwrecked their faith."

1 Timothy 2:1–13:16

- D. Testimony of the truth (2:1–7)
  - E. A word to men (2:8)
    - F. A word to women (2:9–15)
      - G. Church leaders (3:1–10)
    - F. A word to women (3:11)
  - E. A word to men (2:12–13)
- D. Testimony of the truth (3:14–16)

6.D TESTIMONY OF THE TRUTH (2:1–7)

Paul says, "I urge you, *then*" . . . Consequent to charging Timothy to fight the good fight and escape the dangers of a shipwrecked faith, Paul urges Timothy on the paramount importance of sending up prayer and thanksgiving for those in authority, as the curbing of evil aids believers in living quiet and peaceful lives. Prayers for tranquility have God's plan of salvation in mind, and his desire is to save Gentiles as well as Jews the world over. God desires people to come to the knowledge of *the truth*. The truth lies in Christ's ransoming power. The *testimony* of it found Paul being a herald and an apostle to proclaim it.

6.E A WORD TO MEN (2:8)

It has been suggested by one scholar that with the gospel going to the Gentile world (see v.7), and with the church being young there arose the possibility of false teachers spreading erroneous teaching to do with the role of men and women in church. The apostle saw fit for holy menfolk to pray for the aforementioned requests.[2] Yet, the emphasis in Paul's instruction may fall more on prayer than on the subject of men, who are particularly prone to the kind of hindrances to prayer that are mentioned.[3]

---

2. Hendriksen, *Timothy and Titus* (Banner of Truth), 103
3. Fairbairn, *Pastoral Epistles* (Klock and Klock), 121

Says another scholar: generally it is men who should lead in public prayer.[4] *Men* are to lift holy hands in prayer.

6.F A WORD TO WOMEN (2:9-15)

Paul goes to some lengths with instruction for women. Firstly, concerning physical appearance. And secondly, pertaining to submission to men, a submission that historically has been underlined and hinted at in childbirth (see Genesis 3:16). *Women* are to dress modestly. They are to submit to men and learn under them. On the other hand, *women* will be saved through childbirth, and are not be regarded as a nonentity in the church because they give birth to children. They are kept safe and are saved "if they continue in faith, love and holiness with propriety."[5]

6.G CHURCH LEADERS (3:1-10)

This forms the center of the present chiasmus under scrutiny, dealing with the vital subject of those who are to govern congregations. What is to follow by way of spelling out the qualifications of overseers and deacons has apostolic weight behind it because Paul begins: "Here is a trustworthy saying." There is particular solemnity surrounding what Paul has to say.

6.F A WORD TO WOMEN (3:11)

Whether or not we interpret it to mean "wives of deacons" or "women deacons," it is a word to ensure they keep personal confidences. Wives (deaconesses?) are to be *women* worthy of respect.

6.E A WORD FOR MEN (3:12-13)

Taken also with the preceding words addressed to those who may have been deaconesses (vv. 8–10), there are approximately as many words addressed to deacons as to overseers (vv.1–7). The accent is very much on the deacons' domestic lives. A deacon must be a man only of one wife, and have

---

4. *The New Bible Commentary Revised* (IVP) 1171
5. William McDonald *Believer's Bible Commentary* (Nelson), 2085

an orderly home life, since he is responsible in serving (not ruling as elders do) the household of God well in temporal matters.

6.D THE TESTIMONY OF THE TRUTH (3:14-16)

Once more, Paul shows his concern for the truth. With respect to the testimony of the truth and what it has to do with the man Christ Jesus being a mediator between God and men by ransoming men, the actual word "testimony" is not employed here, but the way Christ is said to have manifested himself is attested. Men are to come to a knowledge of the truth (recall v.4), and the church is the pillar and foundation of it, since it not only supports the truth (foundation) but is the pillar where public notice is given by way of added testimony to what Christ has already revealed. [6] The church is strikingly portrayed as God's household, as well as the pillar and the foundation of *the truth*. It is built on the truth as it has been revealed through Christ's testimony to it when He *appeared* in a body, was *vindicated* by the Spirit, was *seen* by angels, was *preached* among the nations, was *believed* on in the world, was *taken up to glory*. Even when he was taken up, his ascension was seen.

1 Timothy 4:1–5:16

  H. Abusing the faith, and marriage (4:1–5)

    I. Training and progress (4:6–8)

      J. A saying of full acceptance (4:9–10)

    I. Training and progress (4:11–16)

  H. Abusing the faith, and marriage (5:1–16)

6.H ABUSING THE FAITH, AND MARRIAGE (4:1-5)

Although there is clear testimony to the truth—just as Paul makes clear in his previous words—he proceeds to reveal that the Holy Spirit expressly or explicitly says some will in later times abandon the faith. The testimony to

---

6. William McDonald, *Believer's Bible Commentary* (Nelson), 2090

Christ is clear, but future abandonment of the faith has been clearly foretold. Herein lies the connection: the little Greek particle *de* indicating the connection between 3:16 and 4:1.

Supernatural forces will deceive some, who will have seared consciences, consciences deadened and without sensitivity towards the testimony of the truth. The Spirit has foretold some will *abandon the faith.* Some will follow deceiving spirits and things taught by *demons.* Among the practices that will be adopted is the command for people not to *marry.*

6.I TRAINING AND PROGRESS (4:6-8)

Even in the present—before the abandonment of the faith comes about—Timothy is charged by Paul to point out the hideousness of abandoning the faith. Much hinges on Timothy himself if he is to influence others for the good. He must train himself to be godly with the realization that godliness has incomparable value. Paul says to Timothy, *"Train yourself to be godly"* —as Timothy teaches *"these things."*

6.J A SAYING OF FULL ACCEPTANCE (4:9-10)

Central in this chiasmus of 4:1–5:16 is a trustworthy saying, that is, one to be taken very seriously, one that has been accepted in the apostolic circle and has become a maxim. Here it forms the basis or foundation for further exhortation to Timothy, which exhortation was to follow the saying, and consolidate and amplify the advice Paul gives the young man according to verses 6 to 8. Donelson somewhere says a trustworthy saying as found in the Pastoral Epistles is the basis or starting point for an exhortation or some application, but he also says it is more like a bridge between what is stated previously and what follows it.

6.I TRAINING AND PROGRESS (4:11-16)

This reflects vv.4:6-8 but, rather than focusing completely on Timothy's personal progress or progress, it touches on the way Timothy is seen publicly among his hearers. *"These things"* is a repeated expression (see v.6), as Timothy is exhorted to point out and teach what is in alignment with truth's testimony. By pointing out and teaching *"these things"* —things centering on the hope we have in the living God (verses 9, 10) —once again however Timothy is told to take heed to himself. No doubt the kind of training to be godly (v.7) is illuminated by what is outlined in the kind of life Timothy leads before believers as their preacher and teacher, he all the while making *progress* and *persevering*.

6.H ABUSING THE FAITH, AND MARRIAGE (5:1-16)

While a new matter becomes the subject for Paul's further instruction to Timothy, some key thoughts return in the letter: to do with abusing the faith and marriage. While much of what appears here is advice about care for widows, a key thought is that care by the church should be exercised if there is no relative who can relieve the church of such pastoral help. Paul has strong words about anyone as a believer, be he or she, who does not provide for a needy relative.

So much for older widows. As for younger ones, they are encouraged to marry, lest Satan gains a foothold for slander. Young widows, as well as older ones, can receive help from believing women in their families so that the church is not burdened and hamstrung in helping those women who have no support among their relatives.

A chiasmus such as that found here in 4:1–5:16 can stimulate serious students of the Word. For instance, a consideration of what drives "hypocritical liars" to forbid people to marry (4:3), and how this appears to contrast with Paul's advice for young believing widows (5:11f). In mirroring passages contrasts and comparisons can be invited. For instance, which is perhaps the more serious if at all of the two and why: abandoning the faith (4:1) or denying the faith (5:8)? Note mirroring has reference to "deceiving spirits" (4:1) and "Satan" (5:15). If anyone does not provide for his relatives, he has denied the faith. Young widows are urged to *marry* again, lest they turn away to follow *Satan*, who is opposed to the Spirit referred to 4:1.

Mirrors in Mark (and in other New Testament Writings)

1 Timothy 5:17–6:21a

- K. Honoring divine trust (5:17–23)
    - L. Good deeds (5:24–25)
        - M. Respect for our superior (6:1–2)
            - N. Wealth and godliness (6:3–10)
        - M. Respect for our superior (6:11–16)
    - L. Good deeds (6:17–19)
- K. Honoring divine trust (6:20–21a)

6.K HONORING DIVINE TRUST (5:17–23)

While the apostle does not emphasize divine trust when speaking of elders at this point, divine trust is implied, for the elders are said to "direct the affairs of the church." (The NIV with some justification has what is dynamically equivalent to "rule," that is, "*direct* the affairs of the church"). The church is the household of God (3:15). The church is to help widows in need, and the church is to support elders out of honor, as "the worker deserves his wages." Elders *who direct the affairs of the church* well are worthy of double honor (the name "Timothy" comes from the word for "honor").

6.L GOOD DEEDS (5:24–25)

After offering advice on quite another matter—making what might be viewed as a relatively unimportant "interjection" in the midst of advice concerning eldership—Paul returns to the issue of elders, showing that even before the judgment to come some sins are obvious while good deeds are obvious too. *Good deeds* are obvious, so that Timothy need not fear that godly, prospective elders will be hard to detect.

6.M RESPECT FOR OUR SUPERIOR (6:1–2)

Paul has been working through the various social groups in the family of faith and now has advice concerning slaves. Nothing is said about masters' treatment of slaves, so that it appears in Ephesus the biggest problem lay in slaves not giving their masters due respect. Slaves are to consider *masters* as worthy of full *respect* or *honor*, believing masters even more so because of the benefits derived.

6.N WEALTH AND GODLINESS (6:3-10)

It is not always the case that the central truth of the chiasmus is the midpoint of it. One must also be cautious at times in claiming one spiritual issue is more important than another but, in the hub of this chiasmus of 5:17–6:21, is a large part devoted to wealth and godliness, larger than the other parts. Wealth, management of finance, and good use of money are often big issues, and contentment together with godliness are to be pursued above all. False doctrine sometimes appears to be a far cry from love for money, but false teachers may often adopt an outward form of godliness in order to make money of religion. Certainly theirs is not a godliness of contentment (v.6), but one of unceasing restlessness in the form of controversies, envy, etc.

6.M RESPECT FOR OUR SUPERIORS (6:11-16)

Timothy is to become free of the entanglements to do with wealth or monetary gain, but it does not come without a fight within. He is take hold of eternal life until our Lord Jesus Christ returns, returning only when God decrees it. God's glorious attributes are spelt out, showing him to be our great Superior, to whom honor and might are due forever. God is the blessed and only *Ruler*. Timothy might well have been called God's slave, but is described here as a "man of God." It was of benefit or *honor* for slaves to serve believing masters (6:1-2), and it is to the *honor* of God if we pursue righteousness, certainly to his honor when Christ returns.

6.L GOOD DEEDS (6:17-19)

Paul returns to the matter of good deeds. In the first mirroring passage of 5:24-25, the advice was taken up mostly with obvious deeds, both good and evil. As well as referring to good deeds again, the apostle speaks not so much to those who want to get rich (v.9) but to those who are rich, urging them to be rich in good deeds, to take hold of true life just as Timothy had been urged to do (v.12). Comparison between the temptations facing those who want to be rich and those who are rich, as viewed by Paul, is worth some study. Also, comparisons made between an elder's good deeds and those of a rich believer can be teased out from Paul's words (compare 5.17 6f with 6:17–19). Those who are rich are commanded to be rich in *good deeds*.

6.K HONORING DIVINE TRUST (6:20–21A)

Paul in his penultimate words to Timothy tells him to guard what has been entrusted to his care. The elders at Ephesus were obviously to take care in the way they governed but based on Paul's words to Timothy, Timothy's work as a kind of sub-apostle had to do with ensuring the elders of Ephesus were of spiritual worth, so that what he was to guard embraced his watch over the eldership. The roles of Timothy and the elders—the interplay between them—is of interest. It calls for study of the whole epistle. Timothy's name springs from the word for "*honor.*" Paul does not word- play upon his name, but Timothy's name can be linked with what was expected of him, and with the honor the elders could attain to (5:17 again).

Benediction and grace (6:21b)

Again, Paul wishes grace upon Timothy.

7

Mirrors in Titus

SOMETIMES THE DIVISION OF chapters in biblical books, as based on a long-held tradition, can obscure the context of a number of passages, and at times the divisions do not blend in with context, but the division of Titus into three chapters, as tradition has it, is quite sound.

Passing over the greeting and benediction at either end of the letter, we are to see there is a common way by which Paul wrote for congregational life (chapter 1), family and individual life (chapter 2), and social and public life (chapter 3).[1] Each kind of life or certain types of persons are brought to Titus's mind, with a reason given for instructing each kind. Hendriksen (see footnote) comes close to identifying the three reasons given; he plainly refers to two of them.

A very common Greek word for "this reason" ("because") is used in three strategic places. The word *gar* is, of course, used elsewhere in the letter, but not often. It is used virtually in those three strategic places at the beginning of each sentence and therefore is emphatic, as it is underlining the reason why Paul is giving instructions to Titus concerning the different kinds of persons or circumstances he has in mind. After stating the kind of elder that ought to be appointed in the church in Crete, Paul states the reason for appointing such a leader (1.10 on), ending with a note urging rebuke. Then, after going on to tell Titus how to instruct various kinds of people in the congregation, he gives what may be called an umbrella reason for such instruction (2:11 on) —a reason applicable to all who have been referred to in 2:1–10—and concludes with a note that lends encouragement

---

1. Hendricksen, *Timothy and Titus* (Banner of Truth), 336

and rebuke. Finally, all believers are referred to in instruction from a public or outside-the-church point of view in Titus 3, and the instruction is followed by the reason for it. (The NIV does not carry the strategic word of *gar* to begin 3:3, unfortunately.) After the reason given, Titus is told to warn anyone who is divisive.

7. TITUS

What constitutes doing good works

Greeting (1:1–4)

    A. Elders to be appointed (1:5–9)

        B. The reason (1:10–13)

            C. Exhortation to rebuke (1:14–16)

    A. The home-circle encouraged (2:1–10)

        B. The reason (2:11–14)

            C. Exhortation to encourage and rebuke (2:15)

    A. Conduct outside the church (3:1–2)

        B. The reason (3:3–8)

            C. Exhortation to warn (3:9–11)

Benediction (3:12–15)

8
Mirrors in Philemon

OUTLINES FOR THIS SMALL letter are usually simple as drawn up by scholars, but there is a chiastic structure within the letter that is a little more complex than in many Pauline letters, and yet the structure is one that lends itself to memorization of the letter's contents.

8. MIRRORS IN PHILEMON

Runaway slave now "useful."
- A. Prisoner with great hopes (v.1a)
  - B. Fellows of various kinds (vv.1b-2)
    - C. Prayer for grace (v.3)
      - X. What was in common, and refreshment (vv.4–7)
        - Y. An appeal in chains (vv.8–12)
        - Y. An appeal in chains (vv.13–16)
      - X. What was in common, and refreshment (vv.17–21)
- A. Prisoner with great hopes (v.22)
  - B. Fellows of various kinds (vv.23–24)
    - C. Prayer for grace (v.25)

85

The mirroring effect in the letter is as follows.

In the "ABC" chiasmus Paul first states he is a prisoner (v.1a), but he has great hopes of acquiring a far more welcome place than a prison—that of a guest room (v.22). Corresponding with those described as a fellow worker and a fellow soldier (vv.1b, 2) are those viewed as a fellow prisoner or fellow workers (v.23). Grace is sought twice (vv.3, 25).

The central chiasmus, and under "X-Y" above, has Paul desiring Philemon to share his faith in fellowship with others who believe, with the apostle recalling that Philemon has already refreshed the saints' hearts (vv.4–7). Paul desires Philemon view him as a partner—two words spring from the same root to do with *fellowship* in both verses 6 and 17—and calls on Philemon to refresh his heart by taking Onesimus back (vv.17–21).

In covering "Y" in the middle of the letter, the chief thought of the letter finds the chained Paul saying Onesimus was once *useless* (a pun on his name) but now he is useful (vv.8–12), and then in chains claims Onesimus is now better than a slave, as he has become a dear brother (vv.13–16).

9
Mirrors in Hebrews

OUTLINES FOR HEBREWS, as drawn up by many scholars, are a fascinating insight into how they see the plan the author of Hebrews had in mind.

One original scholar sees Hebrews not so much as a letter but a sermon that was sent by letter in order to have it read aloud, "probably even performed as a sermon."[1] He argues cogently for this, as the letter contains among other things: cadences of prose rhythm that reflect ancient rhetorical rules, word plays involving assonance (though lost in translation), numerous long and carefully constructed sentences, rhetorical questions, and alliteration. Our scholar claims that no-one listening to Hebrews would have regarded it as a letter, for "the few epistolary elements we have do not come until the end of the document, much too late to signal what sort of document the audience was meant to think it was."[2] Based on all this, he is skeptical of any chiastic structure being detected in Hebrews, saying that there is no way a listening congregation could detect a chiastic structure.

It might well be that a listening congregation could not always detect a chiastic structure, but this does not mean a chiastic structure was not in the supposed sermon. Chiasmi were designed to aid the memory for both the recollection of the written as well as the oral, as the Old Testament makes plain. Hebrew writers also cherished chiasmi when writing. Therefore, if a chiastic structure can be detected in the writing of Hebrews—and it is found in a relatively simple enough form for recollection—then it may be teased out and usefully employed for didactic purposes. Even if the letter had been

---

1. Witherington 111, *Letters and Homilies for Jewish Christians,* 42
2. Op.cit.

originally sermonic in form, listeners could well have been astute enough to perceive in some way or another the chiastic nature of the sermon, not simply for recollection, but for drawing out contrasts and comparisons in the teaching of the deeper truths than those that appear on the surface.

What is central in Hebrews? There have been various outlines suggested to indicate that a number of things are central in Hebrews, but one Jewish scholar contended the high point of Hebrews is found in Jesus being our high priest in heaven.[3] Gentile expositors may find it a little hard to appreciate, but the Jewish expositor, in appreciating the Jewish audience for which Hebrews was written, perceived what the author had foremost in mind. In commenting on Hebrews 8:1, he writes: "Jesus is our High Priest in heaven. This is the crowning point in which all the previous teaching of our epistle culminates." The whole system of priesthood is certainly that which occupies the mind of the author of Hebrews foremost, based on the priesthood being central in Old Testament revelation.

The author of Hebrews in writing, conscious of the required maturity needed for right thinking in order to ensure those believing in Jesus would persevere, reaches the critical stage in his letter by introducing the subject of Melchizedek but hesitates before developing a persuasive theology to do with Melchizedek. Contrary to what John MacArthur says, the author of Hebrews is issuing *a warning* not only to "immature (unbelieving) Jews" but immature *believing* ones.[4] The warning is not as severe as it is for the unbelieving but it is chiefly there for the believing: They are immature and are hesitant about going all out for Jesus. The Hebrew writer accuses them of immaturity but goes ahead all the same to persuade them Jesus is of a higher order of priesthood and they did not need be ashamed to remain clinging to him, unlike their unbelieving countrymen who were still clinging to what must pass away. "Here is the solution of all the difficulties which perplexed the (believing) Hebrews."[5]

A chiasmus need not have the center of it as the most essential matter under consideration, but it may. In Hebrews it can be seen as such.

---

3. Saphir, *Epistle to the Hebrews* (Kregel), 441
4. MacArthur, *Hebrews*, 172-3
5. Saphir, *Epistle to the Hebrews* (Kregel), 442

9. MIRRORS IN HEBREWS

Jesus, our great High Priest
  A. The unchangeable Son and Shepherd (1:1–2:7)

    B. Seeing Jesus (2:8–18)

      C. Faith and the faithful (3:1–11)

        D. Being careful and confident (3:12–4:13)

          E. Priest for perfection (4:14–5:10)

            F. Better things and promises (5:11–6:20)

              G. Our Melchizedekic priest (7:1–28)

            F. Better things and promises (8:1–13)

          E. Priest for perfection (9:1–10:18)

        D. Being careful and confident (10:19–39)

      C. Faith and the faithful (11:1–40)

    B. Seeing Jesus (12:1–29)

  A. The unchangeable Son and Shepherd (13:1–25)

9.A THE UNCHANGEABLE SON AND SHEPHERD (1:1–2:7)

Actually there are here a number of things that mirror those found at the end of Hebrews in 13:1–25, but, of course, Jesus as the Son and the Shepherd is central to both passages, since God has spoken to us through him, speaking through works as well as words. A chief work of Jesus was to provide purification for sin, being superior to angels who are no more than ministering spirits, vital though they be to the believing (1:14), and threatening though they once were to the unbelieving in Old Testament days when their message was "binding" (2:2).

God has *spoken* to *us* by his Son, who provided purification for sin. The creation *will wear out and be changed* as a garment is, but *Jesus will remain the same.*

Angels are *ministering spirits* to inheritors of salvation.

Mirrors in Mark (and in other New Testament Writings)

9.B SEEING JESUS (2:5-18)

The author resumes to speak of the world to come (1:10–13, 2:8), and has in mind that which prevents man from being lord over the earth—the enemy death. He reveals lordship is recovered through Jesus—we see Jesus crowned with glory and honor, becoming a merciful and faithful high priest.

We *see Jesus* crowned with glory and honor. He is bringing many sons to glory. He is *author of our salvation*. We who believe are of his *family—children* of God. He shared *our humanity*. He *suffered* when tempted.

9.C FAITH AND THE FAITHFUL (3:1-11)

Jesus as sent by God is depicted as being faithful. As the Son over God's house he was faithful. "And we [Jews] are his house, if we have courage and hope," says the author. A severe warning against unbelief (unfaithfulness) is to be heeded. *Moses* was *faithful* as God's servant, Jesus as God's Son. Courage and *hope* is what God's people must hold on to. God is *angry* with unbelief.

9.D BEING CAREFUL AND CONFIDENT (3:12-4:13)

Courage and hope is coupled with confidence. Moses led God's ancient people out of Egypt, but God was angry with many of them so he swore they would never enter his rest. Care must be taken to ensure we enter God's rest, only that ultimate rest is still to come—still to come is "a Sabbath-rest for the people of God." The word of God carries promise, yet as spoken by him from whom nothing is hidden.

God is *the living God*. God's people are to *encourage one another daily*. *Confidence must be held firmly* until the end, the confidence that was possessed on *first* believing. There were those who rebelled against God when *Moses* led them out. The Hebrew readers were to be *careful* lest they failed to enter God's rest. There must be *faith*. There is a Sabbath-rest *promised*, as God swore there will be. The word of God is *living*.

9.E PRIEST FOR PERFECTION (4:14-5:10)

Our author with his "therefore" (4:14) is reaching back to where he spoke of Christ having descended and taken on human flesh to be a merciful and faithful high priest (2:14–18). His faithfulness as high priest was directed to God "as a son over God's house" (3:6). In a tour de force, after speaking of the need for believers to have courage and hope so as to be God's house, the author dwells on God's anger and on those who have been denied God's promise of future rest—on the promise still remaining. He also reminds them of the all-searching word of God. The only previous reference to Christ's ascension was indirect and appeared in 2:9, where it spoke of him now crowned with glory and honor.

In speaking of Christ as "a great high priest," it is becoming apparent this is to be a great theme in the letter, a written sermon as Witherington111 perhaps rightly sees it. *Jesus has gone through the heavens* as our great high priest, but unlike the existing Jewish high priests who *offered sacrifices for their own sins, as well as those of the people.*

God *said*, "You are my Son, today I have become your father"; as well as *saying*, "You are a priest forever after the order of Melchizedek."

Jesus, though God's Son, *submitted to God*, was obedient in suffering and was *"once made perfect."* He is the source of salvation for all *who obey him.*

9.F BETTER THINGS AND PROMISES (5:11-6:20)

The author of Hebrews realizes his readers or listeners have been slow to learn. He upbraids them for their sloth, just when he wishes to elaborate on the theme of Christ being an anti-type of Melchizedek. However, he is confident of them understanding, that confidence being based on two things: God will not forget how they have helped and are helping his people, and the appeal to be ever diligent will meet with success as they are God's people. God can be counted on if we anchor our hope in him; the promise to Abraham has been realized in many of Abraham's descendants becoming believers in Jesus, the eternal high priest after the order of Melchizedek.

The would-be recipients of the Hebrews letter are said to be *slow to learn*. Yet *better things* are expected—things that *accompany salvation*. They have been helping God's people. God's promise to *Abraham* came true. God's people's hope has entered *the inner sanctuary behind the curtain.*

Mirrors in Mark (and in other New Testament Writings)

9.G OUR MELCHIZEDEKIC PRIEST (7:1–28)

Here is the heart of Hebrews. While it was vital to establish that Jesus is God, that Jesus is truly human and of Jewish stock, that he is superior to the angels, greater than Moses, it was most essential to reveal how he is like Melchizedek.

Is it an exaggeration to state, "Here is the solution of all the difficulties which perplexed the (believing) Hebrews"?[6] No doubt the portrayal of Jesus as a great and royal priest is central to Hebrews, but only as based on the typology to do with Melchizedek can we see how his priesthood supplants those of the order of the Aaronic one, and shows him to be the one and only eternal priest. It should have provided immense comfort for those Hebrews shy at stretching out their faith to full length for fear of being persecuted by their fellow countrymen, who were still clinging to the Aaronic priesthood in the belief it appeared to be the only valid one. The author reveals why the Aaronic priesthood must now vanish. It carried too many imperfections. Without the author displaying any awkwardness about relying on typology to point to Jesus' eternal priesthood after the order of Melchizedek, the author's audience is expected to fortify their faith in Jesus, not only because the Aaronic priesthood is superseded, but because Jesus' priesthood means he possesses present, ever-present power to save those who come to God through him (Heb. 7:25). Comfort and strengthening there is for those being persecuted or in fear of being persecuted— "He always lives to intercede" . . .

9.F BETTER THINGS AND PROMISES (8:1–13)

After portraying Jesus to be like Melchizedek in that he has an indestructible life—without death preventing him from continuing as a priest—the author reveals Jesus fulfils the prophecy of Psalm 110 and becomes the guarantor of a better covenant.

The Hebrews had previously been said to be slow in learning but, as a skilled and patient teacher, the author of the letter begins 8:1 by saying, "The point of what we are saying is this" . . . Our hope as an anchor enters the inner sanctuary (6:19), which is also *the true tabernacle* where Jesus serves.

Better promises are for those of whom the author expected better things (6:9 with 8:6). Abraham has received what was promised (6:15) in that a new

---

6. Op.cit.

covenant has been made with his people of *Israel and Judah*. Confidence of the author in seeing better things in the somewhat wavering believers (6:9) lies in the knowledge that the new covenant sees *God's laws in believing minds and as written in their hearts* so that they are truly "my people."

9.E PRIEST FOR PERFECTION (9:1–10:18)

Further weaknesses of the Aaronic priesthood are exposed as the author seeks to build up the confidence of his audience. The sanctuary, as well as the sacrifices, reveal the shortcomings under the Aaronic order, and yet it is Christ's sacrifice that is especially considered, after the doctrine of his indestructible life and eternal priesthood had been set forth. His once-for-all sacrifice had opened up the way for believers' perfection and the cessation of sacrifices under the old order.

Christ was formerly said to have gone through the heavens as the great high priest (4:14); now he is spoken of as *having gone through a more perfect tabernacle*, one not *man-made* and *not a part of this creation* (9:11). Aaronic priests continually offered sacrifices (plural – see 5:3), but Christ appeared *once for all* (9:26).

What God *said* with respect to Christ's eternal priesthood is to be noted (5:5–6), and what Christ himself *said* with regard to his intended sacrifice is to be noted (10:5–9).

Christ submitted himself to God (5:7); he *said, "I have come to do your will, O God"* (10:7).

He became perfect through obedience for all who obey him (5:9), and he has *made perfect forever those who are being made holy* (10:14).

9.D BEING CAREFUL AND CONFIDENT (10:19–39)

The emphasis now falls on confidence, though a stern warning is issued in the midst of words of encouragement.

It is stated *"since we have confidence"* . . . (10:19). It is a counterbalance to the earlier word about the need to hold firmly to the end and confidence that was had at first (3:14). *"Let us draw near to God"* . . . (10:22) is seeing in a mirror from another angle the earlier admonition "Let us be careful." (4:1). The Hebrews are also exhorted to *encourage one another* in the light of the coming Day of Christ (10:25), earlier being told to *encourage one another* daily in the light of sin's deceitfulness.

The law or the shepherding of Moses over the people does not occupy the author's mind all that much, since he focuses more on the actual priesthood of the old order in the letter, but there is the reminder of the seriousness of disobeying the law of Moses before Christ (10:28), a warning that dovetails in with the earlier word about the fate of those who rebelled against Moses (3:16). In each of the reminders to do with Moses, the author's audience is called on to reflect that they are dealing most of all with *the living God.*

The confidence that the believers "had at first" revealed itself in *those earlier days after they had received the light, and practiced things that spoke of considerable confidence* (10:32–34). In such light they are urged not to throw away their *confidence*. They are to *persevere*—in other words, hold firmly to the confidence of their early days.

9.C FAITH AND THE FAITHFUL (11:1–40)

Referring already to faith (10:38), our author elaborates on what constitutes faith and how many in the past have lived out their faith. In 11:1–40 we discover what faith is and how it is required of us, with examples of faithfulness following. In the mirroring passage of 3:1–11, examples of faithfulness in Jesus and Moses appear first before faith is defined in terms of courage and hope, and as set against the anger of God towards the hardness of heart. What was stated earlier as incurring the anger of God is counterbalanced in 11:1–40 with what pleases God.

Faith (courage and hope) *pleases* God, and many examples of courage and hope are put forward with the reminder that *the faithful did not receive the things promised* in this life but put their hope in God all the same.

9.B SEEING JESUS (12:1–29)

Jesus is the One on whom we especially fix our eyes, if we accept any discipline that comes our way as God's sons. A warning is issued against missing out on the grace of God, but on the heels of the warning encouragement is given to know that we have as good as come to Mount Zion, the heavenly Jerusalem, which pilgrims of the past longed for. Then again, a warning comes because the future kingdom with the heavenly Jerusalem will not come without a great shaking of the whole earth. On one hand we are to be thankful we have come to Mount Zion, on the other hand we are to worship God with reverential fear for what he intends to do.

Let us fix our eyes on Jesus as *the Author and Perfecter of our faith* (12:2). Already Jesus has been seen as he who is crowned with glory and honor because he suffered death (2:9). He can be seen as the One, who presently crowned, will subject the earth with the Father for full salvation, and he is to be seen as the inspiration for us bearing up under present suffering (see 2:5-9 and 2:18).

Earlier on Jesus is portrayed as an elder brother, bringing many *sons to glory* (2:8-18), yet the glory also embraces *the Author of our salvation* having the Father chastising everyone whom the Father accepts as *a son*. He shared in our humanity (2:14), and we are to *share* in his holiness.

The world to come (2:8) is now defined as *the kingdom that cannot be shaken*.

9.A THE UNCHANGEABLE SON AND SHEPHERD (13:1-25)

Hebrews begins with Jesus viewed as God's Son, offering salvation as Lord (2:2). Such salvation can only be despised with severe consequences. The letter ends by still focusing on Jesus, but not with the angels as ministering spirits in mind (recall 1:14). Rather, ministering agents are now "the (human) leaders," who speak the word of God as deputies for Jesus, and who possess authority as coming from him for obedience. Jesus is still seen among his people, as he is the same yesterday, today and forever. There are leaders but all the same it is Jesus who is the great Shepherd of the sheep.

Angels may be entertained in hospitality, those formerly viewed as ministering spirits (1:14).

Although the world will eventually undergo a change, Jesus had been said to be *the same*, with his years never ending (1:12). He also remains *the same* in the sense that he is the believers' leader whose faithfulness can afford to be imitated.

The letter opens with Jesus at God's right hand after making purification for sins; it closes with him "down here" and "outside the camp," beckoning believers to bear the same reproach he bore. The readers must be brought down to earth, as it were, and reminded we here do not have *an enduring city*, for the world in its present form will perish.

He, who is the unchangeable Son, is the Shepherd to whom be glory *forever and ever* with "years that never end" (again 1:12).

10

Mirrors in James

FEW SCHOLARS ENDEAVOR TO do more than provide a rough outline of James, not considering the structure of it in the possible light of recurring themes.

One scholar has taken some sort of effort to diagnose the structure of James so as to create several forms of parallelism.[1] In much of James 1, for instance, he sees a step-by-step parallelism of A-B-C-A-B-C. Witherington 111 is that scholar who also notes that Frances believes he has discerned a rondo effect in much of the letter. Francis's rondo is somewhat disjointed: It is composed not of chiasmi but, in the main, step-by-step parallelisms with no set rhythms as it were. Also three passages are not embraced by any of the parallelisms so that, whatever rondo there is, it stutters.[2] Witherington 111 discerned that the letter opens with the theme of steadfastness and prayer and then maintains it closes with the same but, strictly speaking, it does not close with the same, as beyond James 5:13–18 are the words of James 5:19–20, which are not necessarily a conclusion in the sense they form a mere end or a finish on the theme of steadfastness and prayer as well. They are divorced as a formal end from the words immediately preceding them. Both Tasker and MacDonald suggest some slightly reasonable but tentative links between 5:13–18 and 5:19–20, so that the letter does not strictly end as it began.[3]

If any structure is to be discerned in James, it must be such that aids the memory. Witherington 111 claims there is a rhetorical structure, on

1. Frances, "Form and Function"
2. Witherington 111, *Letters and Homilies for Jewish Christians*, 406
3. MacDonald, *Believer's Bible Commentary* 142 and, Tasker, *James* (Tyndale Press)

the belief that in Early Church days James the person, as a polished communicator, deliberately used widely acceptable rhetorical skills, but Witherington's proposed structure for James can hardly be rated a mnemonic device. Whatever rhetorical skills might have been employed, James, more than likely, as a typical Hebrew writer, would have styled his letter or written sermon so as to make it memorable, therefore resorting to mnemonic devices such as catchwords or catchphrases. And, as we notice, common in Hebrew writings is the use of chiasmi.

What do we see in James? A mirroring after the chiastic structure of A-B-A seems to be there in a smooth rondo effect throughout the whole letter. Four cycles of A-B-A form the whole letter. Such a suggestion meets the criteria of being relatively simple and aiding the memory about the actual contents of James. Even if James was originally a written sermon, and its chiastic form was in any way lost by some in hearing the sermon, it could have become apparent in the reading of the letter, especially in a Hebrew environment attuned to the constant use of chiasmi in communication.

10. JAMES

The royal law
Greeting (1:1)
  A. Trials and temptations (1:2–8)
    B. The rich and the poor (1:9–11)
  A. Trials and temptations (1:12–18)

      C. Word-doers, faith-workers (1:19–27)
        D. The sin of partiality (2:1–13)
      C. Word-doers, faith-workers (2:14–26)

          E. Words and boasting (3:1–18)
            F. Warning against worldliness (4:1–10)
          E. Words and boasting (4:11–17)

G. An inspiring Old Testament man (6:1–11)

H. No swearing (5:12)

G. An inspiring Old Testament man (5:13–20)

Greeting (1:1)

Although the instruction of James ought not to be lost on any Gentile readers, it is plain that this letter or written sermon was addressed to Jewish or Messianic believers. It helps to explain why this letter may seem enigmatic in parts, but close study of it is rewarding for Gentiles as well.

10.A TRIALS AND TEMPTATIONS (1:2-8)

James is a hard-hitting "servant of God and of the Lord Jesus Christ." No holds are barred. Witherington 111 has many useful insights as to the nature of James's style, his rhetoric, his authoritative way, his deliberative speech being brief and directly to the point, striking out immediately with a strong appeal to the deep emotions of anger and fear and love and hate. Witherington 111 styles the opening words of James as "a preview of coming attractions." Indeed it is.[4]

James tells believing Hebrew Christians to *"count it all joy"* when facing *trials*. Their faith is being *tested*. In such testing they ought to seek the wisdom of God, who is *generous "without reproach,"* but who will not answer those who have two minds about God and do not view him as generously as they should, who have *secret doubts (so unstable)* about whether or not they want God's help.

10.B THE RICH AND THE POOR (1:9-11)

James "introduces another topic" as he proceeds to speak about the rich and the poor believers of the Dispersion. Some view 1:9–11 as yet another topic within James 1:2–25, saying 1:1–25 deals with all the themes that are to be developed in the letter.

It is certainly "another . . . topic"—to be distinguished from what precedes it. Some efforts have been made to weld the words about the rich and

---

4. The whole of Witherington's commentary on James can be read for profit in regard to James's literary style.

poor brothers with the instruction about trials and temptations,[5] but many scholars do not endeavor to weld them. It is such a disruption in thought that the likes of it here in 1:9–11 cause Mitton to claim, "There is in fact no discernible plan in the (whole) epistle"; cause Easton to maintain James lacks any formal plan—not only as a whole, but in its separate parts. May 1:9:11 simply be "another . . . topic," somewhat deliberately unrelated to what precedes it and what follows it? Does James have in fact a formal plan that consists of unrelated topics breaking in throughout the whole letter, sandwiched between four main sections?

Could it not be a rhetorical "trick," that is, while pursuing four main themes, there breaks in between each theme a somewhat unrelated word to catch the reader or hearer with surprise, relieving the mind for a moment of "the one note" being played, and highlighting, albeit for a split second a matter that otherwise may too easily be dismissed? Certainly, an "abrupt word" addressing the matter of the rich and poor strikingly grabs attention briefly, before James resumes to talk about trials and temptations.

10.A TRIALS AND TEMPTATIONS (1:12–18)

Brosend in particular has observed that 1:12–18 bears a clear relationship to the material in James 1:2-8.[6]

James, in resuming to talk of trials and temptations, again refers to trials that put a believer to the test, to see if he is genuine or false. From the root form of "trial for testing" comes the verb for "tempted" in 1:13, so that the same verb that may signify elsewhere "put to the test" is used in a bad sense of enticement to sin, though it is claimed by some the verb ought to be translated "tested." It is better to render it "tempted" since James, in balancing in the main what he previously said in 1:2f, is focusing on the fatal excuse a believer may make in alleging the temptation to sin is too powerful to resist.

Blessed (serving a counterpoise to "consider it pure joy" in 1:2) is he who *perseveres* under *trial*. God has already been seen as *generous*—now it is said every good and perfect gift comes from him. An *unstable man* will not get what he only half-wants—God in contrast is *stable, with no variation due to change.*

---

5. See MacDonald's *Believer's Bible Commentary* and Tasker's *James*
6. Brosend, *James and Jude*, 44

10.C WORD-DOERS, FAITH-WORKERS (1:19-27)

It may well be that there is a link with that of 1:18, in the sense that there follows "practical instructions as to how we can be first fruits of his creatures," that "the word which regenerates brings us under obligation," but it is not strictly true that thoughts about endurance flow on from what precedes 1:18 so that 1:19-20 (and on) has an admonition of "so endure with patience."[7] *Nothing is said of endurance*, except for the brief reference in v.25, for the focus is on listening to the word of God and doing it. Right through to v.27 is the theme of listening and doing, listening and not being deceived.

Believers are to be *doers of the word. A doer who acts* will be blessed. Also, if anyone believes himself to be religious but does not bridle his tongue, "*this person's religion is worthless.*"

10.D THE SIN OF PARTIALITY (2:1-13)

In this the second chiasmus suggested for James, there is a sense in which the fact one must not show favoritism or despise the poor brother is an example of failing to hear the word and doing it, but the theme of the sin of partiality forms a kind of break before James takes up once more the theme of useless religion arising out of the failure to act.

The apostle now deals with a theme that in some ways develops out of the mid-point of the first chiasmus, touching on the matter of those in a "high position" and those in a "low position." Attention is being fixed on the avoidance of snobbery. The motif of shifting from the failure to practice religion, and thus displaying one's religion is useless, to that of treating all believers alike, irrespective of worldly status, fits the royalty we have come to know in Jesus Christ who is glorious. His is a noble name, and the law we are to fulfil is royal and thereby a law that "gives freedom."

10.C WORD-DOERS, FAITH-WORKERS (2:14-26)

Now, James still has in mind the poor in particular (2:14-17) but, more in line with what he said previously about putting into practice what we listen to and not rendering our religion useless, he treasures the somewhat similar theme by relating faith to action. Previously action was described

---

7. Adamson, *The Epistle of James* (NIC on the New Testament) 15

10 Mirrors in James

as arising from listening, not being deceived, not forgetting what we have heard, being truly religious. Such worthy attributes are condensed into what can be called faith to a degree, for faith of course has much to do with what we believe.

James shows there is a belief but it may be only one that causes demons to shudder. It is not a belief in the unity of God and of confidence in him and all his ways; it does not seek to practice obedience to God in heartfelt alacrity.

Faith does not count if it does not have *works* (same word in the original as in 1:25). The *poor* who are poorly clothed and lack food must be given what they need. If not, *what good* is it merely to say "Go in peace ... ?" Previously the exhortation was for the tongue to be bridled (1:26), and now one is cautioned against the empty word from the tongue (vv.15,16).

Religion may be worthless (1:26), faith apart from works is certainly *useless*, as faith apart from works is *dead*.

10.E WORDS AND BOASTING (3:1-18)

There have been some preludes as regard the tongue prior to James 3:1 (see 1:19, 26;2:12), but a new note sounds out here, as the subject now is *taming the tongue*, particularly in reference to teachers or would-be teachers. Words of warning about the tongue will embrace caution against selfish ambition, boasting, judging our brothers in Christ. And for this reason 3:1-18 can be seen as mirrored by 4:11-16. Teachers are mainly under consideration, those who are open to risks in assuming the responsibility of a teacher, those who as a consequence need to live a sound life, "with a wisdom untainted by pride," and so forth. In this way the whole of 3:1-18 can be viewed as related particularly to teachers.[8]

Teachers shall be *judged more strictly*. They are to remind themselves of the way the tongue *boasts* of great things. The tongue is deadly poisonous, for with it *we may curse men who have been made in the image of God*; if we are *brothers*, it ought not to be so. Selfish *ambition* and *boasting* ought not to be harbored in the heart.

---

8. Adamson, *The Epistle of James* (NIC on the New Testament) 16

10.F WARNING AGAINST WORLDLINESS (4:1-10)

James 3:1—4:17 is somewhat like a sonata with its traditional movements of three. There is the exposition (opening up on the common working of the tongue), next the development (enlarging on one of the lines of thought in 3:1–18, that of strife as "a companion of sin,") and thirdly the recapitulation (a return to the subject of caution against an evil tongue). Still, the theme of worldliness in 4:1–10 stands on its own amid the two passages about the tongue. Quite naturally, the tongue features venomously in fighting and quarrelling, but here is a warning against worldliness with a somewhat unparalleled focus on our relation to God himself—as to whether or not we are a friend of God, and whether or not we are personally submissive to him so that he lifts us up.

10.E WORDS AND BOASTING (4:11-17)

Mirroring 3:1–18, 4:11–17 opens up with questioning that reminds us of the former word that: "We curse people who have been made in the image of God. Out of the same mouth came praise and cursing. My brothers, this should not be." Except here it is in the context of being accused of judging the law as well as judging our brother.

The earlier word about selfish ambition and the foolishness of boasting (3:14) is given a practical expression in the caution against presuming one can go to some place today or tomorrow and make a profit on some business, it being labelled as arrogance.

We are not to *speak evil against our brothers*. We are to stand in fear of being judged by him who can save or destroy. It is *boasting* with arrogance to presume we can make plans without considering God's will. *Selfish ambition* may well be betrayed in our words about trading and making a profit.

10.G AN INSPIRING OLD TESTAMENT MAN (5:1-12)

There is a sense in which James 5 can rightly be called a conclusion to the letter in that there is a kind of summary.[9] James 5, however, breaks new ground by dealing with the matter of both patience and prayer through the calling in of two great Old Testament men as a means of inspiration. Under

---

9. Adamson, *The Epistle of James* (Eerdmans), 182

patience Job serves as an inspiration. In prayer it is Elijah. Their examples cannot be over-estimated. Each mirroring part comes to a climax by pointing to the two great men who, though outstanding, serve as ones who can be copied to meet the demands of the day.

The rich have murdered *the righteous person* (ESV). The downtrodden are encouraged to await the coming of the Lord, just as a farmer awaits rain. The brothers are exhorted not to *grumble against one another*. A particular example of suffering patiently is that of *Job* who was rewarded for it.

10.H NO SWEARING (5:12)

Before James returns—so concludes his letter—and re-visits the theme of a great Old Testament man and the inspiration one can reap from recollecting his deeds, he surprises us yet again in a sudden shift to a new out-of-context matter before resuming where he had left off. It has been suggested the matter to do with swearing has a link with what precedes it in 5:1–12 through a theme of judgment, but the link is a little tenuous, because this time judgment is not seen as a threat to those outsiders previously condemned, but to believing brothers.

Witherington says 5:12 "may strike us as an abrupt change of subject," but then claims the themes from 5:12 to the end are in reverse order of those found in 1:2-18. [10] Yet it is hard to find anything to do with oaths in 1:2–18, let alone any other matters of similarity. It seems best to view the matter of "no swearing" as an abrupt change of subject, the kind of thing that has tempted some to believe there is no discernible plan in the epistle.

10.G AN INSPIRING OLD TESTAMENT MAN (5:13–20)

James now dwells on prayer in the main, but he returns to the theme of putting forward a prominent Old Testament figure; this time in order that his readers may be encouraged to meet the conditions for effectual prayer and behold what great things can be achieved by its use.

Patience is one thing (5:1–11), but prayer can avail much in the waiting. Elders can pray effectually for the sick. And instead of lingering on in grumbling against one another (5:9), brothers ought to *confess* their sin as

---

10. Witherington 111, *Letters and Homilies For Jewish Christians*, 539

brother to brother, come clean with each other, and pray for one another. Prayer can be made for healing.

Elijah as a righteous person prayed fervently that it might not rain.

Prayer for each other aids healing, and prayer also takes on legs when we see one of the brothers wandering from the truth and we seek to turn him from his error and rescue him.

11

Mirrors in 1 Peter

IN RECENT TIMES EFFORTS have been made to set forward rhetorical outlines for what has been viewed as a letter that was essentially a sermon—something to be read aloud upon the reception of the letter by the believing Hebrews of the Dispersion. It then appears common to see in the letter first an "epistolary prescript," followed by an "exordium" (introductory part of the sermon). This then is said to be followed by a proposition, which is buttressed by a series of arguments throughout most of the epistle-cum-sermon.

Witherington is one who has championed the cause for the rhetoric and sermonic nature of 1 Peter.[1] He with others looks on 1 Peter 1:3–12 as the exordium for the written sermon, and sees in 1 Peter 1:13–16 the proposition that is shored up with a number of arguments until a "peroration" finally sums up with considerable force what was said. Views differ as to what constitutes the peroration at the end of 1 Peter. It is claimed 1 Peter hinges on the proposition seen in 1 Peter 1:13–16, with key words such as "obedience," "fear" and "holy" pointing to "the theme of this entire discourse (of 1 Peter)."[2]

Well, even though 1 Peter 1:13–16 is prefaced with a "therefore," and "draws a conclusion based on the exordium that precedes it," does it henceforth encapsulate in its brevity all that Peter wishes to say? In a way it does, as it cannot be denied that 1 Peter has much to mention about "holiness of heart and life." It is not certain that Peter's audience would have grasped

---

1. Witherington 111, *Letters and Homilies For Hellenized Christians*, 49f
2. Witherington 111, *Letters and Homilies For Hellenized Christians*, 92-3

that there were five arguments, as Witherington would have it, in support of the proposition—rhetorically-oriented though some recipients of the letter might have been. Still, Witherington and others may have a point, so long as it is recognized that *1 Peter 1:3-12* is seen as just as vital to the substance of what is to follow in 1 Peter. 1 Peter 1:13–16 can well be endorsed only *to a degree* as the proposition for the things to follow in the epistle.

Witherington observes at least one "echo" in 1 Peter, a passage that mirrors another. Without going into the rhetorical base for it, his is an admission of echoing. And could there be more echoes in the epistle? Mirrors? Mirrors throughout the whole letter or sermon?

It might well be that a chiastic structure lies in the Petrine letter that has rhetorical art coming into play also. If 1 Peter is a sermon—and Witherington furnishes cogent reasons for believing it so—then, like any good sermon, it will be rhetorically structured to gain a hearer's ear. And if it be rhetorically structured, repetition of certain words and phrases will appear, so will alliteration, and any manner of word plays.

A chiastic structure to some degree might have been lost on the same hearers, but it may be inherent in the sermon all the same. If the written sermon was circulated—and 1 Peter was widely circulated—the chiastic structure was likely to become more apparent as *the readers* became aware of the strategic places where key words and phrases appear and reappear.

11. 1 PETER

Service and suffering in hope
  A. Benediction (1:1–2)
    B. Suffering a little while for what will not fade (1:3–12)
      C. Self-control, love and the Word (1:13–2:3)
        D. Strangers in pagans' eyes (2:4–12)
          E. Called to suffer for him who died (2:13–25)
            F. A word to wives and husbands (3:1–7)
          E. Called to suffer for him who died (3:8–22)
        D. Strangers in pagans' eyes (4:1–6)
      C. Self-control, love and the Word (4:7–11)

B. Suffering a little while for what will not fade (4:12-5:11)

   A. Benediction (5:12–14)

11.A BENEDICTION (1:1-2)

As Witherington notes, this benediction has "one of the richest salutations in all of the New Testament in terms of theological content." Its theology is rich both in terms of its description of the efficiency of the Triune God for salvation, and in its identification of the ones who were the objects of salvation: the elect sojourners of the Dispersion of the Jews. Right from the start we learn this is a letter for Jewish believers. It was written for believing Jews who lived outside the land of Israel and lived predominantly among Gentiles.

We may add that the salutation heralds what is to be the substance of the letter, that the letter will be occupied with how Jewish believers may cope through living outside Israel their homeland, being encouraged to know all the same they are elect and their inheritance is kept in heaven for them. The letter will center on election and foreknowledge, on the way the Spirit sanctifies God's people, and on how they are to obey Christ who shed his blood for their obedience.

Peter writes to those among the exiled Jews who are *elect*. He writes to those of *Pontus, Galatia, Cappadocia, Asia and Bithynia*.

11.B SUFFERING A LITTLE WHILE FOR WHAT WILL NOT FADE (1:3-12)

The saving work of the Triune God is still in Peter's mind, but it is viewed from other angles. The Father is seen as merciful and the one who causes us to be born again. For "God's vagabonds" there is the hope of an inheritance as Jesus rose from the dead and is coming back. Then the Spirit is referred to: this time as the One who inspired the prophets to foretell Christ's first appearance.

The promised inheritance is *imperishable, undefiled, unfading*. Jesus Christ will *reveal* himself to the praise, *glory* and honor of those who for *a little while* had been grieved by various trials but meet the tests successfully. The Spirit is described here as *the Spirit of Christ* since he is depicted as predicting Christ's coming.

11.C SELF-CONTROL, LOVE AND THE WORD (1:13-2:3)

Peter draws a conclusion from what he said about being born again to a living hope. It calls for action. Action first requires preparing oneself in a sobering way, while keeping in mind the hope of ultimate grace at the return of Christ. Holiness is required, recalling Christ's blood was shed to redeem us from previously futile ways. Just as the salutation succinctly put it: We are to obey Christ whose blood sprinkled us.

There follows an exhortation that embraces the kind of obedience that has in mind love for fellow believers. The exhortation from v.22 on is therefore of a societal nature in the main.

The call is to *prepare one's mind* for action, to be *sober-minded, to love one another earnestly* from a pure heart. It is based on being born again through the living and abiding *word of God*. Love for one another will show itself by putting away malice, etc. The believer's craving for God's Word ought to be like newborns wanting their mother's milk.

11.D STRANGERS IN PAGANS' EYES (2:4-12)

After instructing his readers to live in a holy manner on account of Christ having redeemed them, and exhorting them to love fellow believers deeply, further instruction also has a societal note, only this time it has much to do with believers in their conduct among unbelievers and pagans.

The Jewish believers form the living temple of God, with Christ as the cornerstone. They are a people designed to declare the praises of God in priestly fashion, and to live good lives so that others may glorify God.

The believers are a *people* belonging to God. *Once* they were not objects of mercy, but they are now. They are *strangers* in the world, and are to abstain from sinful desires that *war* against the soul. They are to live good lives among *the pagans* who are ready to accuse them of doing wrong.

11.E CALLED TO SUFFER FOR HIM WHO DIED (3:8-22)

Peter continues to speak of the way one needs to conduct himself in the outside world. Earthly authorities are to be honored so as to "silence the ignorant talk of foolish men." Proper respect is to go out in every direction.

Slaves are particularly addressed, for respect even for harsh masters is expected no less. Inspiration can be drawn from the example of Christ, who suffered abuse without giving in to evil, and who died so that we may die to sin and be led by his shepherding.

Believers—particularly those as slaves under earthly authority to masters—are to realize we have been *called* to endure while under suffering for doing good. It is *better to suffer while doing good* – it being commendable before God. By Christ's wounds we have been healed. He died so that we might die to sins.

11.F A WORD TO WIVES AND HUSBANDS (3:1-7)

The suggested chiastic structure of Peter has at the core of it the words addressed to wives and husbands. This does not mean, of course, these words are the most pivotal in the letter, but simply that they form a bridge before Peter crosses over and continues to go over a theological landscape that is considerably similar to what has already been traversed.

The link between what was addressed to slaves and what is addressed now to wives and husbands is that of instruction for a household. As slaves were of a household, naturally so were wives and husbands, but there is no suggestion that wives were like slaves. Any similarity between women and slaves lay only in being of a household and in a place where "orderliness and deference" are to be expected.

Wives are to be *submissive* to their husbands, even where husbands are unbelievers.

Less is said to husbands than to wives, as Peter needed to define submissiveness closely; he shows that submissiveness has more to do with a beautiful spirit than beautiful clothing and jewellery.

All the same, the words addressed to husbands were meant to be received solemnly.

Husbands are to be considerate, remembering their *wives* are *weaker partners*, though fellow-heirs.

11.E CALLED TO SUFFER FOR HIM WHO DIED (3:8-22)

After the instruction given to husbands and wives, we meet until the final benediction of the letter themes that mirror those that had been seen before, only often in new light or from another angle.

1 Peter 3:8-22 has similar images to those found in 1 Peter 2:13-25, pointing out again the fact that we are called to suffer just as Christ did

when he died for our sins in order to save us, but with new light thrown on what advantage is derived from suffering, and new light thrown on what transpired when Christ suffered.

Once more the link between our suffering and his is established, except now it is a word not merely for believing slaves but for all who believe.

It can be argued that the "finally" of 1 Peter 3:8 stands for a recapitulation of all that had been said before, that is, before 1 Peter 3:8. Grammatically v.9 is one with v. 8, so that harmonious living among the brothers is linked with instruction to refrain from any retaliation. Perhaps the three exhortations of v.8 just pertain to the believing circle, while the three of v.9 have a wider reference, implied by what follows as obvious instruction from Psalm 34 for believers who suffer unjustly at the hands of people of the world.

To this you were called takes us back to 2:21, where the expression is identical. We are called to suffer for doing good. In the first instance, it is regarded as commendable before God (2:20); now it is understood as the means of inheriting the blessing promised in Psalm 34. There is another new emphasis: that of revering Christ, and possessing a calm spirit and clear conscience so as to evoke curiosity about the hope possessed and, if need be, bring down shame.

It is better to suffer for doing good than for doing evil, if it is God's will.

He who bore our sins in his body (2:24) was *put to death in the body* but made alive in the Spirit, the water of Noah's time symbolizing the baptism we underwent and which *saved* through the pledge of a good conscience toward God. (Although the words "healed" of 2:24 and "saves" of 3:21 do not spring from the same root in the original, they invite an interesting comparison.)

New motives are introduced to help weather persecution, and it is evident even believing slaves could also inherit the blessing promised in Psalm 34, as Peter addresses "all of you" (3:8). All could, in keeping with the good conscience obtained upon the pledge made at their baptism, keep a clear conscience in their conduct towards the unbelieving.

11.D STRANGERS TO PAGANS' EYES (4:1-6)

Peter continues to instruct his readers about the way to conduct oneself before outsiders. Here he calls outsiders *pagans*, and it brings to mind the earlier words found in 2:12: "Live such good lives among the pagans . . . "

11 Mirrors in 1 Peter

For Peter is thinking once again of the way believers and unbelievers are strangers to one another. Previously Peter's readers were being reminded that, in becoming God's spiritual house or temple, in becoming his people, in being called out of darkness, they were "aliens and strangers in the world."

There is no explicit recapitulation regarding God's people being a spiritual house, but there is straight-out mirroring through the theme of being socially as strangers to the outside world. As in 2:11–12, the believers are reminded of the need to war against their passions, as that is part of being a sojourner too.

Not only is the mirroring of 2:4–12 seen in the concept of being strangers but in the reaction of the people of the world towards those who had become God's children. The reaction may be seen as twofold—negative and positive.

Negatively, the pagans or Gentiles are depicted as accusing God's people of doing wrong according to 2:12, and the mirroring sees them as heaping abuse on God's people according to 4:4. So maligning of the brothers takes on two forms, malignity being viewed from two different angles.

Positively, a mirroring may be seen in 2:12 and 4:6. Admittedly, both verses have been open to controversy and open to more than one view, but it is being suggested here that "the day of visitation" (2:12) is when God visits certain detractors who come to their senses and are saved, and that also the preached gospel of 4:6 meets with success in some so that those saved, and who have died, now "live according to God" in their spirit.[3]

With respect to 2:12, we may add to Stibbs's comments by stating that the good works witnessed by those visited by God to their salvation are to be linked with the fact that God's people may prove convincingly to be a royal priesthood in declaring the praises of him who called them out of darkness into his marvelous light. Deeds and declaration help make for a change of mind by some when God visits them.

Indirectly, the theme of God's spiritual house (2:4–10) is acknowledged in 4:1–6. Being declarers of praise of God through declaration and deeds, words and works, leaves them open to abuse, but is also the means for some finding salvation—expressed in 1 Peter 2 in terms of God visiting them, and in 1 Peter 4 in terms of the gospel being preached to them effectually.

God's people are to *arm* themselves against sin, which means to war against sinful desires in the soul (see 2:11 for comparison). The Gentiles think it *strange* that God's people no longer plunge themselves in sin as they

---

3. Stibbs, *The First Epistle General of Peter*, 108, 151

did once. *Enough time* had been spent doing that, when once they were not God's people (see 2:10).

The Gentiles heap abuse on them.

The gospel was preached to the believing who now are dead. In their lifetime they were judged by their opponents and condemned. Yet since death, in the spirit they are beyond the clutches of their adversaries and live unto God.

11.C SELF-CONTROL, LOVE AND THE WORD (4:7-11)

This episode begins with what may be rendered as : "But the end of all things is near". Peter is emphasizing the nearness of the end, and we find him appealing to his readers in much the same way as he did formerly when he spoke about the grace that is coming to us "when Jesus Christ is revealed". Formerly, as the NIV has it in 1:13, Peter told his readers they were to prepare their minds and "be self-controlled so that you can pray".

A mirroring is witnessed in this cluster of images to do with the thought of loving each other. Each time the admonition is to love one another deeply (1:22, 4:8), except in 4:7-11 love is more closely defined: love encompasses the practice of hospitality; as covering many sins; embraces the use of our gifts for one another; speaking the very words of God if so gifted; and also serving in God's strength.

Believers are urged to be *clear-minded* and *self-controlled* in view of the end of all things being near. Formerly, such action was urged in order to set one's hope on the coming grace at Christ's revelation (1:13) — now, such kind of action is urged for the reason of prayer.

Believers are to *love one another deeply.*

Grace may be present here and now in service to one another, while awaiting the grace yet to appear at Christ's revelation.

All are born again "through the enduring and living word of God" (1:23), and yet there are those who can administer God's grace in service to others by teaching spiritual truths, speaking *the very words of God*, thus inviting interesting and edifying comparisons to be drawn from the twin themes to do with the word of God—it having regenerative power, and being used by the gifted to speak to the believing for their sanctification.

11 Mirrors in 1 Peter

11.B SUFFERING A LITTLE WHILE FOR WHAT WILL NOT FADE (4:12–5:11)

In the suggested chiastic structure of 1 Peter, this penultimate passage contains a lengthy portion of the letter, but hardly any more than what appears on either side of the midpoints of the letter in 2:13–25 and 3:8–22. The important thing to grasp is the mirroring of 1:3–12 in 4:12–5:11.

The theme of suffering certainly pervades the whole of the Petrine letter, but what makes a mirror here for 1:3-12 are the images of suffering and joy together, of joy and glory and suffering as well.

The Spirit is only referred to in the whole letter in both 1:3–12 and 4:12–5:11. Earlier on he is depicted as "the Spirit of Christ," here as "the Spirit of glory and of God."

More could be teased out from the references to the Spirit, but we move on to contemplate "glory to be revealed" even in instruction to elders (5:1), such glory reserved for all tried and true believers "when Jesus Christ is revealed" (1:8). All believers enter the inheritance that "can never fade" (1:4), but there is a hint that a particular "crown of glory will never fade away" in the future for faithful elders.

Then there is a final word that actually forms a benediction (vv.10–12) with a phrase unique to both 1:3–12 and 4:12–5:11—about suffering *for a little while*.

There are all kinds of trials (1:6) but suffering unjustly at the hands of those who insult us is particularly *painful*. Still, one can *rejoice* at the thought of Christ's *glory being revealed*. Moreover, even when we suffer, *the Spirit* of glory and of God rests on us.

Elders will receive a crown of glory *that will never fade away*, the assurance given by Peter who is certain he will share in *the glory to be revealed*. God is one of all grace and, after we have suffered a little while, he will restore us to his glory.

11.A BENEDICTION (5:12–14)

The letter closes with an acknowledgement of Silas, who helped Peter write the letter. Silas was not merely a deliverer of the epistle, but helped to write it in a style acceptable to Hellenized Christians,[4] doubtless with

---

4. See Witherington 111 in *Letters and Homilies for Hellenized Christians*

Peter's peculiar experiences as an apostle to stamp the letter with apostolic persuasive words that would leave his readers standing fast in God's grace.

The letter had gone out to the Jewish believers of the Dispersion, to certain provinces of what is now western Turkey. Did it originate in literal Babylon, as some suppose, or does Babylon stand for Rome? As a codeword does it stand for the center of organized godlessness? If a cryptic name, it could suggest exile in the great capital of Rome itself, and reflect Peter's call for steadfastness in the godless center as a means of inspiring all Jewish believers who must sojourn outside their homeland of Israel to remain true to the God of all grace.

Yet, there is good reason to believe the letter was sent out from Middle Eastern Babylon: the order of the countries mentioned at the beginning of the letter is such as would be adopted by Peter writing from actual Babylon. The province mentioned first is Pontus—nearest to Babylon. Then is a southward movement the others are referred to in circular fashion through to Bithynia.

Peter and Silas had written the letter. It was written for *the chosen* from *Babylon* to the places referred to at the letter's opening. Peace is wished for all the believing readers.

12

Mirrors in 2 Peter

WITHOUT DELVING TOO MUCH into the complexity concerning the authorship of 2 Peter, of the way it came to be written, and of the similarity to Jude in the second chapter, it can still be considered in terms of some chiastic structure. It has been said that word-wise only 38 percent of its vocabulary is repeated.[1] In the light of such slim repetition of vocabulary, one might think that conforming 2 Peter to any chiastic structure may be Procrustean.

Yet, chiasmi may be discerned in this letter, resting not only on phrases or words that are strictly identical, but on themes that see various passages bearing similarity to others within the epistle. For instance, chiasmi may link up two words such as exploit (2:3) and entice (2:18). Strictly speaking, "exploit" and "entice" are not the same in meaning—*exploit* standing for "making use of unfairly," and *entice* for "attracting by offering pleasure or advantage"—but they carry some connection when both passages embrace these words to depict the methods employed by false teachers when they move in so as to catch believers off guard. The motives behind exploitation and enticements are also highlighted in those episodes. Yes, and another theme—and still to do with condemnation of false teachers—is highlighted in the two passages even nearer the center of the chiasmus of 2 Peter 2: the theme of Old Testament cases of condemnation of apostates.

---

1. Witherington 111, *Letters and Homilies for Hellenized Christians*, 260

12. 2 PETER

Always remember

2 Peter 1

    A. Promises and prophecies (1:3–4)

        B. Making every effort (1:5–9)

            C. Being more eager (1:10–11)

        B. Making every effort (1:12–15)

    A. Promises and prophecies (1:16–21)

2 Peter 2

            D. Exploiting and enticing (2:1–3)

                E. Past cases of condemnation (2:4–10)

                    F. Those going the same way (2:11–14)

                E. Past case of condemnation (2:15–16)

            D. Exploiting and enticing (2:17–22)

2 Peter 3

            G. Apostolic reminder (3:1–9)

              H. The day of the Lord God (3:10)

                I. What we ought to be (3:11)

              H. The day of the Lord God (3:12–13)

            G. Apostolic reminder (3:14–18)

SALUTATION (1:1–2)

Like the salutation of 1 Peter, it heralds what is to be the substance of the letter: in this case it hints that the kind of righteousness which was instrumental in the readers receiving a precious faith will make for a home

12 Mirrors in 2 Peter

of righteousness when the new heaven and the new earth appear (3:13), which future home as a prospect ought to stir the readers into living holy and godly lives now (3:12f). Much is also made of knowledge of God and of Christ in the letter (1:3, 5, 8; 2:20; 3:1, 2, 8, 15, 16, 18). That which Peter prays for on behalf of his readers—grace and peace—he himself supplies in part, as the letter is replete with knowledge through reminders and further enlightenment about the things that spell out salvation.

2 Peter 1 (after the salutation of 1:1–2)

   A. Promises and prophecies (1:3–4)

      B. Making every effort (1:5–9)

         C. Being more eager (1:10–11)

      B. Making every effort (1:12–15)

   A. Promises and prophecies (1:16–21)

12.A PROMISES AND PROPHECIES (1:3–4)

Peter continues on from his greetings to speak of knowledge of God, that it is a knowledge accompanied by power for godliness, as well as being accompanied by precious promises.

God's *power* has been given for godliness, calling us according to his *glory* and goodness. Moreover, he has also given us very great and precious *promises* to participate in the divine nature and escape the corruption of the world.

12.B MAKING EVERY EFFORT (1:5–9)

For reasons that have been given, through power and promises the readers are urged to make every effort increasingly to possess such qualities of spirituality so as to be productive in their knowledge of our Lord Jesus Christ. Paradoxically, standing still spiritually means going backwards, one could say.

Make every effort, says Peter, to be productive in knowledge of Christ, so as not to *forget* what was first known.

12.C BEING MORE EAGER (1:10-11)

Eagerness is urged all the more to make our calling and election sure, not only because of prospective productiveness, but because lack of productiveness means becoming near-sighted and forgetting the reason for having been cleansed. The prospect of being welcomed into Christ's kingdom must be kept in mind.

12.B MAKING EVERY EFFORT (1:12-15)

Peter now turns attention to the effort he himself is making to ensure his believing readers will not forget what he has told them, since soon he shall die and desires that his words will keep ringing in their ears after he has gone.

Peter would remind them of what can be forgotten if one becomes near-sighted and blind to what one had first seen (1:9). What was made clear to Peter by Christ he desires to make clear to his readers. As well as the readers making every effort for salvation, he himself will *make every effort* to help them *remember* what he told them.

12.A PROMISES AND PROPHECIES (1:16-21)

Prophecies are promises of a kind. Peter turns to what he and John and James witnessed when Jesus appeared in glory and honor as the Son of God on the Mount of Transfiguration. The Old Testament prophets had predicted Christ's coming in power and great glory in what can be called promises. It appears the ancient Scriptures confirmed the apostolic witness. No contrast by way of value is being drawn between the Scriptures and Peter's experience. The Scriptures put a stamp on what Peter and his two companions witnessed. Michael Green believes "(Peter) is saying, 'If you don't believe me, go to the Scriptures.' "[2] The Scriptures were a witness.

Jesus Christ's coming was with *power*. The prophecies (*promises*), as coming from men of God, confirmed and made sure that what the apostles said was true.

---

2. Green, *2 Peter and Jude*, 86-7

12 Mirrors in 2 Peter

2 Peter 2

    D. Exploiting and enticing (2:1–3)

        E. Past cases of condemnation (2:4–10)

            F. Those going the same way (2:11–14)

        E. Past case of condemnation (2:15–16)

    D. Exploiting and enticing (23:17–22)

12.D EXPLOITING AND ENTICING (2:1–3)

The apostle proceeds to show that, like false prophets of old, false teachers will arise to trouble the believers. The ancient false prophets had claimed to be true prophets at times with signs, and in that way perhaps were to be distinguished from the false teachers among the apostle's readers, but at least they had in common the power to deceive.

The false teachers deny *the Sovereign Lord who bought them*. They are dangerous, for they can *exploit* people with stories that are made up – cleverly invented stories that Peter had no part of when he spoke of the Transfiguration (1:16).

12.E PAST CASES OF CONDEMNATION (2:4–10)

Destruction for false teachers is not sleeping. Condemnation fell on the evil ones of time past, therefore destruction is inevitable for the current false teachers. Three examples are given of judgment and two of deliverance. As for deliverance, the saving of Noah and his family, and the rescue of Lot, serve as an inspiration for Peter's godly hearers. Note the particular attention given to the case of Lot.

In a triad our author shows God did not *spare* certain angels, did not *spare* "the ancient world," and *condemned* Sodom and Gomorrah to fire. Lot *lived among* the wicked but was rescued.

12.F THOSE GOING THE SAME WAY (2:11-14)

False teachers are going the same way as the condemned of old. They are noted for their contempt for authority. Their brazen ways are depicted. Ironically they even challenge celestial beings but will die as the beasts they are.

12.E PAST CASE OF CONDEMNATION (2:13-16)

That the false teachers will be "paid back with harm" is further substantiated by Peter providing even more evidence of their evil ways, that to some significant degree they resemble the ways of Balaam of old. Balaam was covetous, as well as influencing God's people for immorality. A mere dumb beast restrained Balaam—even the simplest believers should perceive the blatant evil of the false teachers though they are painted with deceptive, seductive sheen.

The believers' cloaked-enemies *feast with the believers*—Lot of old lived among those destined for destruction. *Balaam* is a prototype of enemies they face, but they are to recall he was *rebuked* (thus condemned) for his wrongdoing in his madness by a donkey.

12.D EXPLOITING AND ENTICING (2:17-22)

As if enough had not been written about the false teachers, the apostle through sheer weight of words depicts the emptiness of the seducers, and their tactic of seeking to entice the newly converted with false promises. This is followed by an explanation as to why they are as evil as they are, couched in language that harks back to what was previously said about them denying the Sovereign Lord who bought them—in the sense of defining how such a denial eventuated.

If it were not for the weight of words to do with the nature of the false teachers and the predicted destruction of them, the seriousness of their power to seduce would be belied.

Although "empty" of any merit, the false teachers are able to *entice* the newly converted. They themselves may have appeared at first as newly converted, but their initial escape from the world's corruption through a knowledge of Christ only led them to be entangled by the world's corruption so that through denial of Christ *they became worse at the end than they were at the beginning*. In this way they denied the Sovereign Lord who had

appeared to have bought them. All along they were dogs—now going back to their vomit. All the time they had been pigs—washed but returning to wallow in the mud.

2 Peter 3

    G. Apostolic reminder (3:1–9)

        H. The day of the Lord God (3:10)

            I. What we ought to be (3:11)

        H. The day of the Lord God (3:12–13)

    G. Apostolic reminder (3:14–18)

12.G APOSTOLIC REMINDER (3:1–9)

Once again Peter indicates he is reminding them to keep alive to the things of salvation. He draws attention to the fact that both letters were written to stimulate wholesome thinking, though the second letter is not occupied with the dangers inherent in persecution but with the dangers inherent in the deceit practiced by false teachers. In becoming acquainted with the two letters of 1 and 2 Peter we learn dangers lurk in both open lion-like attacks and the sly and snaring lamblike ways.

One more issue needs to be dealt a death-blow before the apostle closes his letter: that of the jibe of scoffers who will maintain that the believers' hope of a Second Coming is hollow, and that creation shows no signs of possible divine intervention. The matter of exploitation and the moves of enticement made by the false teachers are left behind as adequately dealt with, to focus on creation and why things seem deceptively to be as they always were. Yes, reference is made to scoffers saying what they think about creation as based on evil desires, but the apostle does not let the matter lie content with that, since he is out to encourage his fellow believers, who may become unsettled by the scoffers' reasoning. Three times in the remainder of the letter Peter calls his readers "beloved" as he meets seriously the contention of the scoffers.

Future tense is employed to speak of the scoffers' arrival. Witherington surmises that it is possible the scoffers' arrival signals to Peter that the very end was at hand.[3] Witherington sees it ironic that those who deny the end of the world are perhaps living near the end of it! The scoffers were already present among the readers but the holy prophets of old, together with Jesus' apostles, had given prior warning of the scoffers' appearance, hence the use of the future tense. So it was not necessarily signaling the very end.

It may be that even such words as Peter's in his first letter—1 Peter 4:7—inadvertently gave rise to the jibe "Where is this *coming* he promised?" Peter defines in this the second letter what is meant by the end being "near." Any assertion that Peter believed he and his hearers were living near the very end of time is dubious, when one reflects on the apostle's insight into God's sense of time and God's patience until all the elect are saved (vv.8,9).

Peter says by *letter* he is reminding his readers of certain things. Scoffers will come and *deliberately forget* what God did in the days of the universal Flood. Believers are not to forget God's sense of time and God's *patience* until all believers are saved.

12.H THE DAY OF THE LORD GOD (3:10)

The Day of the Lord may be delayed but when it comes, it shall come suddenly as a thief. The world will be destroyed, just as it was in the days of the Flood—not destroyed so as to be completely obliterated but destroyed in the sense of being "cleaned up" in readiness for God's plan of restoration of the earth. The Day of the Lord will be more cataclysmic than the Flood, as the renewal will be more radical in its effect—the earth is to be a lasting home of righteousness (v13).

The Day of the Lord will see *the heavens* disappear, *the elements* destroyed, and everything "laid waste and totally plundered," in keeping with the prophecy of Isaiah 24:3.

12.I WHAT WE OUGHT TO BE (3:11)

A moral imperative follows the description of the future cataclysm. Rarely if ever do we find in apostolic writings that the nearness of death is a motive for godly living and its future reward: the pervading motive for such is Christ's Return.

---

3. *Letters and Homilies for Hellenized Christians.* 371

12.H THE DAY OF THE LORD GOD (3:12-13)

It appears there is toggling with the identity of the One whose Day is coming. Jesus is titled "Lord and Savior" in v.2, presumably "the Lord" of v.8 is God. Is the Lord of "the Day of the Lord" the Father or the Son? In v.12 the Day is described as "the Day of God," and then simply "that Day" in v.12b. When we recall Jesus is called "our God and Savior" at the beginning of the letter with grammatical justification, we may be at a loss as to the definite identity of the one whose Day is coming. It may have been of little concern to the apostle, viewing God and Christ so closely in purpose that if the distinctions seem blurred, it is of no consequence.

That Day will see *the heavens* disappear (v.10) in the sense of being destroyed, will see *the elements* destroyed by fire through melting in the heat. The earth will be totally plundered so as to make way for a home of righteousness—it will be plundered of its wickedness. It will be plundered, for it had been stated earlier that the Day of the Lord will come like a thief.

12.G APOSTOLIC REMINDER (3:14-18)

Peter had earlier said the readers were to look forward by "holy and godly lives" to the new heavens and the new earth (v.12). In somewhat similar language he now urges the brothers that if they are "looking forward" for this, they should make every effort to be found "spotless, blameless and at peace with him." "Make every effort" has been urged twice before (1:5, 15).

As the author nears the end of his letter, not only does he inspire his readers to "look forward," but backs his authority for believing God's patience signifies a delay of "that Day" by enlisting the support of "our dear brother," who wrote on similar lines, and whose writings are considered as Scripture. Then, once he points out how the Pauline, sacred writings are also taken lightly by "ignorant and unstable people" to their destruction, he closes the epistle with a final imperative to not only to be on guard but also to "grow in the grace and knowledge of our Lord and Savior Jesus Christ."

Paul also wrote *letters* to do with *God's patience for salvation*. Just as scoffers are said to come and follow "their own evil desires," and will deliberately forget the judgment of the Flood in Noah's day, so "the ignorant and the unstable" are said to *distort* the difficult parts of Paul's writings. Paul's literary works are on the level of "the words spoken in the past by the holy prophets and the command given by our Lord and Savior through your apostles"—those *"other Scriptures."* The *"dear friends"* are not to be carried away by the error of *lawless men*, earlier defined as a deliberate forgetfulness born out of evil desires. *Our Lord and Savior* had given a command concerning the emergence of scoffers, and he is the One spoken of as *"our Lord and Savior* Jesus Christ" when we are urged to grow in grace and knowledge. "To him be glory both now and forever. Amen."

13

Mirrors in Jude

As is well known, Jude and 2 Peter bear remarkable similarities to one another, and yet the structures of both are quite different. Certainly from a chiastic viewpoint they are different, even though only three verses at the beginning, and seven verses at the end of Jude, do not have extensive parallels with 2 Peter.[1] Still, within what look like parallels between them, there are considerable differences between what Jude omits or includes, thus allowing for a chiastic structure to differ between Jude and 2 Peter.

There is soundness in holding that after the greeting of Jude 1–2, the short letter can be divided into Jude 3–16 and Jude 17–23, the former spelling out the reason *why* one must contend for the faith once delivered, the latter spelling out *how* one is to contend. Jude 3–16 is occupied with description of the apostate teachers and the way they operate, while Jude 17–23 fixes on the resources one can fall back on in order in order to combat the apostate teachers.

Still, such a twofold division is to be viewed as a too simplistic device to impress the reader's mind. There is a more mnemonic and vivid way to impress one with much of what the letter actually contains.

Dr Coder once had published in *The Moody Monthly* many years ago what a scholar called Richard Wolff described as a "structural outline for Jude"—a chiasmus actually.[2] The chiastic scheme presented below coincides more or less with that found in Wolff's commentary of old.

---

1. Green, *2 Peter and Jude*, 50
2. Wolff, *A Commentary on the Epistle of Jude*, 34

Wolff actually made no use of Coder's chiastic structure in what was otherwise an excellent exposition of Jude. Below appears what strengthens much more of the foundation of that which Coder put forward as a structure by also pointing out the actual catchwords and catchphrases that serve as mirrors in Jude.

13. JUDE

On contending for the faith

   A. Service and authority (v.1a)

      B. On being kept (v. 1b)

         C. Mercy (v.2)

            D. The Faith (v.3)

               E. Denying and dividing (v.4)

                  F. Ancient warnings of punishment (vv.5–7)

                     G. "These dreamers," "these blemishes" (vv.8–10)

                        H. Ancient trio of apostates (v.11)

                     G. "These dreamers," "these blemishes" (vv.12–13)

                  F. Ancient warnings of punishment (vv.14–16)

               E. Denying and dividing (vv.17–19)

            D. The Faith (vv.20–21a)

         C. Mercy (vv.21b–23)

      B. On being kept (v.24)

   A. Service and authority (v.25)

13.A SERVICE AND AUTHORITY (V.1A)

Coder placed Jude 1 and 2, and Jude 24 and 25, under the umbrella of "The security of the believer" but, in the mirrors of the aforementioned verses that signify the beginning and the end of the letter, there are more

13 Mirrors in Jude

distinctive features to be observed than Coder noticed, features that contribute better to the reflection of the beginning and the end.

Jude (known as "Judas" in Matthew and Mark) begins his letter with one of his favorite literary devices—that of triplets. The triplet in v.1a is: "Jude," "servant," "brother." Although a brother of our Lord, he humbly designates himself as "a servant of Jesus Christ," and pays homage to his well-known brother James.

Jude is a *servant* of Jesus Christ.

13.B ON BEING KEPT (V.1B)

Once again Jude adopts his literary device of triplets to impress on our memory the importance of what he has to say. The triplet here is: "called," "loved" "kept." In the original the emphasis is on him who loved us and who as a consequence made us by Jesus Christ "kept-called" ones.

The stress lies on being kept by the Father and Jesus Christ, as the work of being kept is viewed as a vital thing in the light of much that is said about the dangerous apostles.

The readers needed assurance of their secure, salvific position, just as the letter discloses.

Jude writes to those who are loved by God the Father and who are being *kept* by Jesus Christ, as they were called to be *kept*.

13.C MERCY (V.2)

"Mercy" is alongside "peace" and "love" in forming a third triplet, and it heads the list. A profitable comparison can be made with the mercy exercised divinely in response to a prayerful wish for present mercy (as here) and that later enjoined by Jude in vv.21–23.

Mercy, peace and love in multiplication are wished for.

13.D THE FAITH (V.3)

This can also be viewed as "the believer and the Faith" (Coder), and is mirrored by v.20. The believers are being urged to contend for the body of truth and divine revelation that is unchanging (note in contrast that the apostates "change the grace of God into a license for immorality"—v.4). Most of Jude is occupied with an identikit of the apostates and their evil.

For some Jude's letter may seem unsavory for modern taste but, in Jude's eyes, contending for the faith means knowing your enemy well and realizing how treacherous he is—this forms a sizable part in being equipped to contend for the Faith.

In a change of mind, due to the pressing and urgent circumstances facing the believers, Jude states he has written to urge them to contend for *the Faith*.

13.E DENYING AND DIVIDING (V.4)

Here forms the actual beginning of detail concerning the deadliness of the apostates' ways and teaching.

Yes, another triplet appears. This time: "slipped in," "change," "deny." The ESV renders the three verbs as: "crept in unnoticed," "pervert," "deny." The three verbs aptly describe the reason for certain men having preordained condemnation hanging over their heads. Ungodliness characterizes what they are doing.

Certain men, whose condemnation *was written about long ago*, are godless and have slipped in among the believers unnoticed as those who pervert God's grace *and deny* Jesus Christ.

13.F ANCIENT WARNINGS OF PUNISHMENT (VV.5-7)

The triplet of "those who did not believer," "the angels" and "Sodom and Gomorrah" covers a history that Jude's Jewish readers are acquainted with, but made vivid in recollection by the triplet, as Jude reveals how condemnation has already fallen on certain ones in the past. The triplet takes us back to the unbelieving among those of Israel in the early days, then up to the celestial realm of the angels, and finally down again—to the heathen cities and environs of Sodom and Gomorrah. Wolff graphically states: "Even the best-known truth is not so well known that it may not be better known." To help make it better known Jude employs the triplet technique.

We are to note as well that, in the use of the triplet, the condemnation is outlined in the three forms it took. The unbelieving Israelites met physical death in the desert, the angels are chained in darkness until the final judgment, Sodom suffered earthly fire symbolic of eternal fire.[3]

The unbelieving Israelites were *destroyed*. The rebellious angels *have been kept in chains in darkness*. Those of Sodom *are an example of those who suffer the punishment of eternal fire*.

13.G "THESE DREAMERS," "THESE BLEMISHES" (VV.8-10)

After revealing that ancient warnings of punishment are awaiting the apostates through proof of what actually took place long ago as punishments, Jude returns to the theme of "the certain men" he had warned the believers about before. He enlarges not on the way they have slipped in but on what had become an open, brazen way of displaying the immorality previously mentioned, of the form that their rejection of authority takes (recall v.4). Rejection of Christ's authority as the only Sovereign and Lord surfaced in rejecting also celestial beings, even daring to do what Michael the archangel was afraid to do.

The triplet in v.8 of "pollute," "reject" and "slander" becomes a device to point up a similarity to the despicable immorality and rebellion in the past in Sodom and among the angels, but most of all points forward to the daring slander that characterizes the false teachers.

These dreamers are daring in "the daylight." *These* men speak abusively of what they do not understand—like unreasoning animals. Destroyed by the very things they say and do.

13.H ANCIENT TRIO OF APOSTATES (V.11)

At the midpoint of Jude (if one views the whole letter chiastically) stands the three examples of individuals who were apostates of the past but who have their imitators in the present apostates that come under Jude's condemnation. Cain, Balaam and Korah form a triplet to underline the evilness of evil (to borrow a Hebraic way of speaking).

These three apostates in various ways met their doom not too long after they committed their sin, and the present apostates will not meet it until the Lord returns. However, they are as good as judged already, since they

---

3. DerBerefJuda, R. Stiera, *Verlag von Hertz* (Berlin, 1850)

have taken the course that leads to judgment. The "woe to them" anticipates the misery and suffering that is bound to come.

13.G "THESE DREAMERS," "THESE BLEMISHES" (VV.12–13)

After fixing readers' minds on judgment during the days before Christ came, the passage that here mirrors the words of vv.8–10 has the expression "these..." at the beginning of the description of the apostates to emphasize the present reality of apostasy threatening the community of believers.

Having exposed the apostates' presumption to dare to do what the archangel Michael refused to do (vv.8–10), and pointing out in succession the damnation of Cain and Balaam and Korah, Jude shows up the apostates as an actual danger among the brethren, elucidating on what he said earlier about these men secretly slipping in among them. It would have been easy for the believers to downplay the evil of the apostates since the believers were rubbing shoulders with them at the love feasts, consequently it was not enough to brand them simply as shepherds who only feed themselves, but to expose their barrenness and emptiness by drawing on four invective similes to reinforce the certainty of future judgment.

Jude deviates from the practice of triplets so as to jolt his readers with a quadruplet of similes to do with the world of nature so that they may steer clear of the false teachers' influence.

"*These* men are blemishes at your love feasts"

13.F ANCIENT WARNINGS OF PUNISHMENT (VV. 14–16)

Building on the previous word about the people of Sodom and Gomorrah serving "as an example of those who suffer the punishment of eternal fire," Jude recalls Enoch prophesying of the Lord coming with his holy ones to execute judgment "on everyone." Even the angels are bound with everlasting chains for "judgment on that great Day." The angels are bound for "the great day," Sodom and Gomorrah are pointers to that great Day, and Enoch prophesied concerning it. Both vv.5–7 and vv.14–16 reflect warnings through example and prophecy about the Lord coming to judge everyone.

God's people who did not believe perished soon after deliverance from Egypt. Rebellious angels still remain bound for the great Day, which Enoch prophesied about. Sodom and Gomorrah are reminders the Lord comes to *judge everyone*, all the ungodly who ever lived.

13.E DENYING AND DIVIDING (VV.17-19)

Coder has this passage mirroring that of v.4, for both have to do with "Apostates described." One can see that much of Jude is replete with description of the apostates, so is there anything unique to justify mirroring what is here and what is in v.4? What they have in common is the description of the way the apostates invade the believing community. Subtly they change the grace of God into a license for immorality, doubtlessly subtly dividing the believers who would perhaps be at loggerheads with one another over the acceptability of certain ones—deciding or judging among each other as to who had the Spirit and who did not. The imagined superiority of the apostates would bring on wrangling even between the true believers about the degree of tolerance and discernment required.

Both episodes uniquely refer to the Lord Jesus Christ in reference to the invasion of the apostates. Both foretell the fate of the godless men, who deny the Lord Jesus Christ and divide his people.

The apostles of *our Lord Jesus Christ foretold* the day of scoffers, of the men who *divide* the believers. Using an excuse for immorality (v.4) is a form of following mere natural instincts.

13.D THE FAITH (VV.20-21A)

In contrast to those who scoff, who divide the believers and who follow mere natural instincts, those who are brothers in Christ are admonished to do certain things to avoid the contamination of the false teachers.

While in the original, the emphasis of v.20 falls mostly on the believers keeping themselves in the love of God, Cranfield rightly observed: Verses 20 and 21 form one sentence, which, in the quadruple exhortations given, the first and second and fourth are subordinate to the third one of "keep yourselves in the love of God."[4] The Berkeley Version did well in translating.

"You, however, beloved, as you build yourselves up upon your most holy faith and are worshipping [sic] by the Holy Spirit, *keep yourselves in the love of God* [italics mine], all the while awaiting the mercy of our Lord Jesus Christ for eternal life."

It is the catchword "faith" that lends reflection to v.3. New here is that the faith—the body and truth of God's revelation—"that was once for all entrusted to the saints" is considered subjectively a holy faith, the readers'

---

4. Cranfield, *1 & 11 Peter and Jude*

own holy faith. Previously consideration was given to contending for the body of faith, and now the faith is what the believers are to build themselves up on. Witherington suggests that building oneself up in the faith is to be equated with contending for it. In Jude such building up seems an antidote for any contamination by the apostates, as curiously nothing is said about excommunication of the godless by the community of faith.

As a means of keeping themselves in the love of God, those *loved* by Jude are to build themselves up in their most holy *faith*.

13.C MERCY (VV 21B-23)

Although the phrase "as you wait for the mercy of our Lord Jesus Christ [to bring you] eternal life" is subordinate to "keep yourselves in the love of God," the link with what follows in vv.22 and 23 is apparent. And *mercy* is a catchword that mirrors that which is found in v.2.

The mercy in mind in v.2 and v.21b is a divine exercise, in the first instance something sought for in this present age as a divine favor, in the second instance something to come in with the new age under Christ's Kingship. In the first instance it is something prayed for, in the second that which we wait for.

As Jude begins to close his letter, the mercy now in mind is a human exercise, one presumably practiced towards the apostates or those coming under their spell. Jude indulges in the use of a triplet once more, as appropriately he advises his readers on a final note about the way to rescue some from the danger of apostasy. As a true doctor of the soul, he perceives that in the attempt to save any, conditions or symptoms vary from one case to another. Some are in two minds about false teaching, some are caught up in the error and need to be snatched from it, some have abandoned themselves to it and we cautiously need to pity them.

It is profitable to compare or contrast divine mercy with human mercy, as Jude portrays them.

Wait for the *mercy* of our Lord Jesus Christ to eternal life. Be *merciful* to doubters. Snatch some from the fire of false teaching. Be *merciful* to others with the utmost caution, without sympathy for their sin.

13 Mirrors in Jude

13.B ON BEING KEPT (V.24)

Even though there are two different words employed for *keep* at the beginning and the end of Jude, they are a part of the mirroring effect in the letter that requires more refinement than simply terming verses 1–2 and verses 24–25 as "The Security of the Believer" in the way Coder did.

Strong maintains that the first *keep* used by Jude has to do with watching and guarding from loss or injury, whereas the second *keep* stands for prevention from escaping. The first word, he says, is suggestive of watchful care over a present possession, whereas the second one indicates safe custody and often implies assault from without.[5]

In the first instance (v.1) we are said to be kept by, or for, or in Jesus Christ—kept by the calling He issued to us. In the second instance the keeping has to do with God viewed as Savior and who through Jesus Christ our Lord is able to keep us from falling until he brings us "into his glorious presence without fault and with great joy." We recall that earlier on Jude admonished us to keep ourselves in the love of God as well.

Benediction salutes God our Savior with the ability to *keep* us from falling.

13.A SERVICE AND AUTHORITY (V.25)

Jude at the outset had described himself as "a servant of Jesus Christ." At the end of the letter we are reminded that among other things, God our Savior is to be ascribed *authority* through Jesus Christ our Lord. Servanthood and authority go hand in hand to serve the cause of contending for the faith.

Jude's letter has its humble beginnings with him styling himself as a mere servant of Jesus Christ, but his letter carries considerable authority because he is a servant of *Jesus Christ* who is Lord and who through God is Savior. The letter is ever ascending in tone. It moves from urging readers to contend for the faith for the sake of not satisfying the ungodliness of some who have invaded the community of believers. The letter further ascends by establishing that condemnation has been foretold concerning apostates, then to the consideration of "the Lord...coming [eventually] with thousands upon thousands of his holy ones to judge everyone." Contrast is then made between what the ungodly are doing in divisiveness and what believers need to do for assuring themselves of God's love and the carrying

---

5. *"The New Strong's Exhaustive Concordance of the Bible"*

out of merciful acts to save others. Lastly, a great height is reached with the focus on the time when God's great presence will be known, the assurance being that in this present age he is at work to achieve that end, with all honor going to him through Christ.

God is Savior and therefore all glory, majesty, power and authority through Jesus Christ our Lord will deservedly go to him eternally.

14

Mirrors in Revelation

WHILE APPRECIATING THE MANY attempts at the outlining and subdividing of Revelation as made by scholars down the years, and without denying there is a definite step-by-step scheme behind the formation of the Apocalypse, it is worthwhile to consider the possibility of viewing the book in terms of the symmetry of a large chiasmus.

Mirroring is obviously seen in both the passage of the letters to the seven churches (Revelation 2–3) and its reflecting passage that tells of the descent of the New Jerusalem to earth (21:5-22:6). The letters to the seven churches and the narrative of the descent of the New Jerusalem are linked by a number of catchwords or catchphrases such as "overcomes," "the second death," "the new Jerusalem." While a number of these catchwords or catchphrases may also appear outside the passages of both the letters to the seven churches and the description of the New Jerusalem's descent, nowhere else in Revelation do they appear in such a cluster. It is noticeable too where both the aforementioned passages appear: one near the beginning of Revelation and one near the end.

Does such inverted parallelism run through the rest of the book? The outline below demonstrates that it does, so that a chiastic structure is discernible to the point where the episode of the beast arising out of the sea and the beast coming out of the earth form the center of the Apocalypse. If the Apocalypse is chiefly concerned with End Times and what is to occur just prior to the Second Coming of Christ, we expect that the unparalleled antichristian forces to come will be much focused on by John. It will not seem strange to think the passage of both the beast arising out of the sea and the beast coming out of the earth forms the literal center of the book.

Yet, if there is a definite linear-scheme in the drawing up of Revelation, how can it accommodate a chiastic structure as well? Was a chiasmus also deliberately woven into the book? As shown previously in the introduction to this volume, Kenneth Bailey reveals how chiasmi subconsciously have long been practiced universally. It may well be—probably is—that the chiastic structure behind Revelation just "fell out" the way it did when the step-by-step scheme behind the book was being formed. There is evidence of biblical inverted parallelisms being quite deliberately employed in the Old and the New Testament, but it does not mean that all of them were so.

Still, the author of Revelation may have been aware of reaching the climatic point in "seeing" the beast coming out of the sea and also the beast coming out of the earth. Then in reaching "the point of turning," the author realized that the rest of what he was to "see" would introduce crucial new elements that linked up, resolved, or completed the first half of what was revealed to him. The climax had been reached in the vision of the Antichrist and was to be followed by the taking up of the previously-known clusters of catchwords and catchphrases of Revelation 1–12 in order to employ them in more advanced settings beyond Revelation 13 for truth already revealed.

14. REVELATION

"Come, Lord Jesus"

- A. The testimony (1:1–3)
  - B. Alpha and Omega (1:4–8)
    - C. Falling down to worship (1:9–20)
      - D. Overcoming (2:1–3:22)
        - E. The dwelling of God (4:1–11)
          - F. Reigning on earth (5:1–14)
            - G. White horse, white clothing, world rulers (6:1–17)
              - H. Salvation of God (7:1–17)
                - I. Seven intense judgments (8:1–9:21)

        J. Completion (10:1–11)

          K. The temple (11:1–19)

            L. Salvation and judgment "have come" (12:1–13:1)

            M. The two beasts (13:2–18)

            L. Salvation and judgment "have come" (14:1–13)

          K. The temple (14:14–20)

        J. Completion (15:1–8)

      I. Seven intense judgments (16:1–18:24)

    H. Salvation of God (19:1–10)

    G. White horse, white clothing, world rulers (19:11–21)

    F. Reigning on earth (20:1–15)

  E. The dwelling of God (21:1–4)

D. Overcoming (21:5–22:6)

C. Falling down to worship (22:7–11)

B. Alpha and Omega (22:12–17)

A. The testimony (22:18–21)

14.A THE TESTIMONY (1:1–3)

Revelation is declared to be a revelation God gave Jesus Christ. This simple matter can easily be lost in the common eagerness to identify the Beast and things of that nature. The revelation is also to be seen as that which is disclosed by Jesus Christ himself, therefore we read an angel went to John from Jesus Christ, whom God gave a revelation of things to come, John in turn through Jesus showing God's servants these things.

    Such things are to be shown by reading aloud what is written. John is thinking of the hour when his book will be read by the lector in each of the churches.[1] The whole revelation will have already been written down by the time God's servants have heard it read, with blessing being promised to reader and listener.

Testimony as a word appears 12 times in Revelation but, here and in the reflecting passage that ends the book, it is specifically associated with reactions to the reading of the words of the prophecy of the book, and the nearness of the time of Christ's Return.

The testimony

12.1 The revelation of Jesus Christ is given to show what must *soon take place*. John *testifies to everything* he saw by way of vision. Blessing is assured to the reader and listener of the things John saw, since *the time is near*.

14.B ALPHA AND OMEGA (1:4–8)

Salutations go out to the seven churches of Asia from John with the desire that grace and peace be upon them, the grace and peace that comes from all in the Trinity, each of whom is described in a way that is fitting according to what is found in Revelation. Jesus Christ receives the fullest portrait because he is the One who bore a faithful witness to the things on earth and who then rose from the dead, and who is bound to be the ruler over the earth. Moreover, it is through him that we, who are the object of his love and the focus of his deliverance, will also reign as kingly priests when he comes again to judge the world, which judgment we believers are to give our assent with a "So shall it be! Amen."

It is natural to deduce that the first person mentioned for the grace and peace that is to come on the seven churches is actually God the Father (v.4, seen in terms of "Him who is, and he who was, and who is to come"). He who later declares himself to be "Alpha and Omega, who is, and who was, and who is to come, the Almighty" (v.8) is plainly recognized as "the Lord God." The other members of the Trinity are not described as him "Who is, and he who was, and who is to come," though they are eternal as well.

Before John received his first vision, "he was given a reaffirmation of God the Father's sovereign lordship over history."[2]

1. Lenski, *St John's Revelation*, 33
2. Ladd, *A Commentary on the Revelation of John*

Alpha and Omega

12.2 Greetings go out to the seven churches of Asia. Grace and peace is sought from *him who is, and who was, and who is to come*; from *the Seven Spirits*; from *Jesus Christ*, the One destined to be *ruler* over the earth. Jesus is the One who shall make his people *a kingdom and priests*. The Lord God affirms this shall be so, as he is *the Alpha and Omega, who is, who was, and who is to come.*

14.C FALLING DOWN IN WORSHIP (1:9-20)

Significantly, the first vision John sees is that of Jesus. He appears "like a son of man." What John sees is to be written on a scroll and sent to all seven churches of Asia, so awesome is the sight of Jesus, an awesomeness to be weighed up solemnly when each church receives a letter peculiar to them becoming overcomers in their unique circumstances. Jesus (his human name) appears as the risen Lord and appears in imagery reminiscent of that found in Daniel, where one "like a son of man" arrives on the earth via the clouds of heaven to use his invested authority, glory and sovereign power to reign universally with a kingdom that shall never end. Therefore, the allusion to Daniel is not accidental to the book of Revelation.

Jesus' greatness overwhelms John so that he falls at Jesus' feet "as though dead." John is told not to be afraid. Jesus is the Living One who holds the keys of death and Hades.

He is told to write down what he has seen, what is now, and what is to take place later.

Falling down in worship

12.3 Upon seeing Jesus in all his authority, glory and sovereign power, John falls at his feet to worship him. Jesus tells him he has no reason to fear.

Then, he is bidden to write *"what you have seen, what is now and what will take place later."* In other words he is not to seal up the words of the prophecy of the book.

Mirrors in Mark (and in other New Testament Writings)

14.D OVERCOMING (2:1–3:22)

The whole seven churches are to receive on a scroll what John saw of Jesus in his risen and exalted state, but each church is to receive a letter to address the circumstances they find themselves in.

The predominant word to the seven churches is *overcome*. Outside the letters to the seven churches, *overcome*, with its allied tenses, is found in Revelation only at 12:11, 17:14 and 21:7. Its unique use in the seven letters lies in the compass of exhortation and promise. As for Revelation 21:7, it lies within the very passage that will mirror 2:1–3:22. Each church is inspired to overcome, having a promise stretching before her as a fillip to withstand the temptations and trials that beset her.

All the churches were situated in the Roman province of Asia, in what is now Turkey. From the island of Patmos, where John was imprisoned, a courier could have made a circuitous route to deliver the seven letters, beginning with Ephesus and ending at Laodicea. That there were seven churches as recipients of the letters suggests divinity and a desired perfection in devotion within the seven assemblies and the congregations in their area.

The pattern of the seven letters is unique apart from the structure that has to do with any chiastic features within the rest of Revelation. There is a chiasmus within a chiasmus. The pattern within the framework of the seven letters is as follows -

A. "Repent" and "love" (church in Ephesus)

   B. "Synagogue of Satan" (church in Smyrna)

      C. "A few things" (church in Pergamum)

         D. A compromising assembly (church in Thyatira)

      C. "A few people" (church in Sardis)

   B. "Synagogue of Satan" (church in Philadelphia)

A. "Repent" and "love" (church in Laodicea)

Each of the letters to a large measure open with a spelling out of the various attributes Jesus displayed in the first vision John received and as they are related to the particular situations each assembly was in. And as far as prospects were concerned, appealing peculiarly to each church. Frequently the end of each letter spells out the prospects coming to fruition once the

New Jerusalem descends at the end of the present age. Therefore, each letter looks back and looks forward in the bid to have every church overcome and inherit what is promised.

Overcoming

12.4 Overcomers in the church at Ephesus are promised the right to eat from *the tree of life*. Those in Smyrna are promised escape from the peril of *the second death*. A white stone will be given to the victorious of the church in Pergamum. As for the faithful in overcoming at Thyatira, Jesus pledges to give them authority over the nations. No names among the overcomers at Sardis will be erased from *the book of life*. In *the temple of God* the victorious at Philadelphia in the future will be pillars. Then those of Laodicea, if overcomers, are given the pledge of sitting down with Jesus on his throne, a throne distinguished from Jesus' Father's throne, the throne he shares with the Father in the present time.

All *overcomers* are promised the inheritance of all that pertains to the descent of the New Jerusalem to the renewed earth (21:7).

14.E THE DWELLING OF GOD (4:1–11)

John is bidden in the second vision to "come up here" and sees what "begins the veiling of *what must take place after this*."[3]

John is on the edge of seeing the beginning of judgments on the unbelieving world at large, and of viewing the attempts made by the unbelieving world to hunt the believers down to extinction.

That the word *church* is not heard of again in Revelation in the coverage of the events leading down to and including the End Times, does not mean the church will have disappeared. There is no further need for John to employ the term "church" after Revelation 3, since he has finished with the notion of believers gathered together in assemblies here and there. Moreover, there is sufficient disclosure in Revelation 2–3 to transport us into "what must take place after," and for us to well imagine—without the term "church" later being employed—how the church will fare as a whole in the perilous times beyond the era of the listed seven churches of Asia.

---

3. See *New Bible Commentary Revised (IVP)*, 1287

In other words, the letters are futuristic and point beyond the era of the seven churches.

Revelation 4, together with Revelation 5, forms "a general introduction to the opening of the Seals and the solemn events of End-time."[4] It is a crucial general introduction to understand the necessity for John to go up into heaven to witness the sovereignty of God and to learn what his will is for the universe. God as Creator is a doctrine not to be underestimated. Hence John views God gloriously enthroned, though curiously "the One who sat on the throne" is not exactly named—it all adds to the mystery of his being.

John has mystery unfolded before him, not only seeing the One on heaven's throne, but watching four living creatures and 24 elders who are lost in wonder and praise of the Sovereign's holiness and worthiness.

John learns that by God's will all things were created and have their being.

12.5 John looked, saw a door to heaven open, heard a voice as of a trumpet say, *"Come up here."* There appears a *throne in heaven*, around which gather four living creatures and 24 elders, before which throne also are the Seven Spirits of God.

14.F REIGNING ON EARTH (5:1-14)

Again God is described as the One who sits on the throne. As King, the future of creation must by necessity be fashioned according to his will.

The scroll given to the Lion of Judah speaks of a testament or a will, containing inside what makes for a divine inheritance for the world's people, God's ransomed people to be exact. The inheritance became available on the death of one who had power to make the inheritance possible, but his shed blood is also seen in terms of a *ransom* as well.

The earth is the inheritance. Those who are ransomed by the blood of the Lamb shall serve God and reign on the earth as a kingdom and priests. Proleptic language of the present tense is used in anticipation of what will definitely occur when Jesus brings in his kingdom. His throne is future (see 3:21), and to be distinguished from that of the Father's.

---

4. West, *The Thousand Year Reign of Christ*

Reigning on earth

12.6 A scroll is given to the Lion of Judah, the Davidic ruler to come. The scroll enshrines the will and testament concerning the inheritance of the earth. A ransom had been paid to secure the inheritance. Both the four living creatures and the 24 elders burst into song at seeing the Lamb take the scroll, the song reaching its climax on a note that spells out both the will of God and the intent of the Lamb in ransoming God's people:

"You have made them to be a Kingdom and priests to serve our God, and *they will reign on the earth.*"

14.G WHITE HORSE, WHITE CLOTHING, WORLD RULERS (6:1-17)

It has been put forward by Ladd that the Lamb was given a scroll that had seven seals on the outside edge, that the breaking open of all seven seals preceded the exposure of the contents of the scroll.[5]

The scroll contains all the rest of Revelation, from the first seal down to the coming of Christ, down to the millennium and the descent of the New Jerusalem. For upon the seventh seal being opened, there appears the revelation of the trumpets. The seventh trumpet, when blown, ushers in the seven angels with the seven plagues that complete the wrath of God on earth before the kingdom of Christ takes effect and before other events that follow on from the coming of the kingdom.

The breaking of the first seal symbolizes what is discovered in the scroll about a rider coming forth on a white horse. Who is the rider? It could hardly be the Lamb, as he is the One who is opening the seals. All the same, the rider has something to do with the cause of Christ, as the whiteness of the horse suggests. It appears to stand for the conquering gospel, with the next three seals depicting the unsettling of a world that attempts to put down stakes to secure itself against the conquering power of the gospel.

Yet, there are believers who will suffer to the point of death, becoming scapegoats in time of war, famine and the rest. As martyrs they cry out for vengeance in heaven. The reply comes in the form of white robes and being told to wait a little longer until the whole number of martyrs is completed.

The only places in Revelation where "white horses" are referred to are in Revelation 6 and 19, in passages that mirror one another by also

5. Ladd, *Revelation of John* 79-80

referring to white dress and "the kings of the earth." The kings of the earth appear at the opening of the sixth seal, when a description of events leads us to the threshold of the end, when kings and people of all walks of life fear at the shaking of the heavens and the quaking of the earth.

White horse, white clothing, world rulers

12.7 One of the four living creatures calls forth the first of the four horsemen to come—the rider comes on *a white horse*. With the coming forward of the four horsemen, martyrdom will result. The martyrs are given *a white robe* to wear—symbolic of some blessedness of purity until the end. *The kings of the earth, the princes, the generals, the rich, the mighty,* and the rest of men will, like the martyrs, call out for help, only towards the end those unbelievers will be calling out for the mountains and rocks to fall on them in dread of the great day of divine wrath.

14.H SALVATION OF GOD (7:1-17)

Revelation 7 is parenthetical. Before the seventh seal is opened, before "the beginning of the proper end" (Klicfoth), before the consummation as distinguished from the culmination of the sixth seal (Lange), before the prayers of the martyrs for vengeance are answered (Nathaniel West), we are made to realize who can stand on the great day of God's wrath (6:17). Who can stand? Two groups of people: those comprising the saved of ethnic Israel and those comprising the church characterized largely by Gentiles. Or, to put it another way: Those numbering 144,000, and those without number.

Regarding the 144,000, it is not entirely pertinent to the work of seeing mirrors in Revelation to make a full-sized defense of reasons for believing the 144,000 represent ethnic Israel, but only to claim that "Israel" means "Israel," "the tribes of Israel" means "the tribes of Israel," and that it is unimaginable to think a book about End Times would not touch on God's promises of the restoration of Israel and the re-installation of the Davidic kingdom on earth.

With respect to the "great multitude that no one could count" (v.9), it must be seen as a number largely Gentile, "from every nation, tribe, people and language." It is a number distinguished from that of "all the tribes of Israel" (v.4).

14 Mirrors in Revelation

It is in Revelation at the point of describing the great multitude in white robes where that which is mirrored quite extensively later in 19:1–10 is seen.

Salvation of God

12.8 John says he saw *a great multitude before the throne and in front of the Lamb*. These are they who, when martyred and gone to heaven, have cried out with a loud voice for vengeance. Now they have more than white robes—they hold palm branches in their hands, since victory is certain and their prayers are to be answered.

They cry out, *"Salvation belongs to God."* The elders and the four living creatures fall down on their faces before the throne and worship God. And they cry out, *"Amen!"* Those who come out of the great tribulation *serve* God day and night. Never again will they *hunger* or *thirst*.

14.I SEVEN INTENSE JUDGMENTS (8:1–9:21)

At the opening of the seventh seal there is silence for half an hour, for the seven judgments to follow are most intense. The prayers of the martyrs (see 6:10) are to be answered. The signs foreshadowing the coming wrath of God and of the Lamb (see 6:12–17) have gone unheeded. Calamities step up in severity from what was witnessed under the seals, going from one quarter of the earth being affected to one-third.

The first four trumpets affect the world of nature, the last three are more direct judgments on men. The traditional divisions into chapter 8 and chapter 9 conveniently demarcate the two kinds of judgment. The four judgments affecting the physical or natural world serve as a warning of the other three to come (C.Y. Bliss). It will be hell on earth from then on (C.Y. Bliss again).

Evil supernatural beings will rampage the world, doubtlessly producing a chill among the sealed of God, but the sealed of God (recall Revelation 7) will be sheltered by divine protection.[6]

---

6. Ladd, *A Commentary on the Revelation of John*

Mirrors in Mark (and in other New Testament Writings)

Seven intense judgments

12.9 *Seven angels* appear with seven trumpets. *The first angel* causes judgment to fall on *the land, the second on the sea, the third on courses and bodies of water, the fourth on the heavenly bodies, the fifth inflicts great agony* on men, *the sixth* helps to set loose four angels bound at *the River Euphrates* so that a third of mankind meets death. The rest still *refuse to repent of their evil.*

14.J COMPLETION (10:11)

Before the sounding of the seventh trumpet, there is inserted an account of a vision of a great angel,[7] who comes down from heaven with a little book in his hand. To this is added parenthetically the account of the measuring of the temple, as well as the ministry and death and ascension of the Two Witnesses. All this in Revelation 10:1–11:14 is an interlude before the sounding of the seventh trumpet.

John is forewarned that the prophecies, which are related to the sounding of the seventh trumpet as issuing into the seven last plagues, will be sweet to taste but bitter to digest, since the last plagues will be an even more severe judgment than those of the trumpets.

The seven thunders suggest "there are dimensions of reality which man is not able in this life to contemplate,"[8] thus John was forbidden to record what the seven thunders said.

The angel swears "by him who lives forever and ever" that the mystery of God is to be accomplished upon the sounding of the seventh trumpet. John's prophecies to come will concern "many people, nations, languages and kings." Although the book that the angel gave John may seem to have been "little," it contained what is to concern many peoples.

Completion

12.10 John hears *seven thunders* but is forbidden to write what he heard. The angel swears by him *who lives forever and ever*, saying that it is definite that *the mystery of God will be accomplished*. John eats the little book,

---

7. See G.E. Ladd's cogent reasons in his commentary on Revelation for not believing the great being is Christ

8. Boer, *The Book of Revelation*

discovering it is *sweet as honey to the mouth* but *bitter to his stomach. Many peoples, nations, languages, and kings* are to be prophesied about.

14.K THE TEMPLE (11:1-19)

Two temples receive recognition when John continues to prophesy. One is of the earth and relates to God's ancient people of Israel being destined to be protected at the advent of the Seventh Week, which Daniel prophesied about. The other temple is found in heaven, where the Ark of the Covenant is seen amid grave signs of the coming judgment on earth.

The trampling of the holy city of Jerusalem by the Gentiles, who assume control of the outer court of God's earthly temple, seems to refer to the first half of the Seventh Week of Daniel, that is, refer to the first 3½ years. Then in the middle of the seven years, "the beast that comes up from the Abyss will attack (the two witnesses)," and kill them, breaking a covenant with God's ancient people, as predicted in Daniel. The beast will woo the whole world into condemning the two witnesses, the world joining the beast in gloating over their deaths.

The last woe to fall on the world is soon to come.

The sounding of the seventh trumpet inaugurates the kingdom of the world becoming the kingdom of God and his Christ. This is proleptic language, things couched in language to express the "as good as done," for actually the kingdom of the world does not become the kingdom of God and his Christ, and come into full effect, until the seven bowls of God's wrath are poured out on the earth, when "God's wrath is completed" (15:1), and when the seventh angel has poured out the last of the seven bowls and the loud voice from the throne exclaims, "It is done!" (16:17).

In concert with the seventh angel blowing the seventh trumpet of warning and loud voices exclaiming that God's kingdom has come, the 24 elders worship God and say, "Your wrath came" (the ESV correctly has it as past tense). This is said proleptically, as the dead will not be judged (v.18) until the thousand years of Christ's reign is completed (Revelation 20). That will be the time when the destroyers of the earth meet their ultimate and utter destruction (v.18 with 20:11-15).

Mirrors in Mark (and in other New Testament Writings)

The temple

12.11 *The temple of God* on earth is measured to put the boundary between those who worship God in truth and those who do not. The outer court of the temple—the court of the Gentiles—symbolizes the apostasy in *the holy city* of Jerusalem among those false to God in Israel and resemble those who are unbelieving Gentiles. *The great city* will be under the Beast's control.

The seventh angel with the seventh trumpet causes loud voices in heaven to proclaim God's Kingdom has come. The 24 elders respond, *"God's wrath* came." The time *had come* to judge the dead. *Earth's destroyers* will fittingly be destroyed.

14.L SALVATION, JUDGMENT "HAVE COME" (12:1-13:1)

John will proceed to reveal in what way the believing of Israel will be protected. Protection will be sorely needed since the world will come under the spell of an enraged Satan, who loses what power in heaven he possessed and who comes down to vent his spleen on the faithful of God. Satan knows his time is short. He goes after those of the whole race of Israel first, but on finding she (Israel) is beyond his clutches, he "makes war against the rest of the offspring (of the woman with the crown of 12 stars)."

David Stern asserts the rest of the woman's offspring are Gentile Christians,[9] but more than likely by "the rest" is meant those who are also offspring in Israel as Christ was, and who believe.

Salvation, judgment "have come"

12.12 A woman clothed with the sun appears in heaven. She has twelve stars for a crown. Satan as a dragon seeks to devour Christ, who was of Jewish blood. The woman flies to the desert, to a place of divine protection. An enraged Satan loses any authority he had in heaven. He is cast down to the earth.

The ejection of Satan from heaven actually signals *"Now have come the salvation and the power and the Kingdom of our God,"* as his ejection is a sign that the end is near.

Yet the faithful need not be alarmed. By the blood of the Lamb they overcome Satan, and by *the word of their testimony* as well.

9. *Jewish New Testament Commentary*, 826

Jewish believers are also said to *obey God's commandments and hold to the testimony of Jesus* (v.17).

14.M THE TWO BEASTS (13:2-18)

The episode concerning the two beasts is not mirrored elsewhere, for it forms a midpoint of the whole chiasmus behind Revelation. It stands solitary in a sense. Being the midpoint, it does not necessarily form the heart of the book, but it takes high place in the events pertaining to the end, since "the beast out of the sea" in particular is a dominant figure in the struggle for the supremacy of the world. The two beasts are terrifying agents on earth in Satan's final days of warfare against God's people.

Just as Israel once sang by the Red Sea "Who is like You, O Lord, among the gods", so the world's worshippers will exclaim "Who is like the beast?" (S.P. Tregelles).

The beast of the sea is referred to in Revelation 11 rather briefly, but upon John seeing in vision more completely the beast arising out of the sea, it features largely in the remainder of Revelation, until he is viewed as cast into the lake of burning fire, once Christ returns victorious to the earth.

This passage forms more than a casual reference to the beast—he had only been viewed in passing previously (11:7f). The midpoint is pivotal to an understanding of the high pressure believers will stand against in the last days, and what unbelievers will buckle under rather helplessly but deservedly. The last days will be a time calling "for patient endurance and faithfulness on the part of the saints" (v.10), but it will see the world astonished by the first beast's power, and also see the world eager to follow him through the demonic persuasiveness of the second one.

14.L SALVATION, JUDGMENT "HAVE COME" (14:1-13)

Passing the midpoint of Revelation, the mirroring of all that preceded Revelation 13 comes into play.

In reflecting 12:1-13:1, the subject of 14:1-13 in part circles around the 144,000 who appear victorious on Mount Zion with the Lamb. They are the ones earlier viewed as the rest of the offspring of the woman clothed with the sun and crowned with seven stars on her head. They are with the Lamb on Mount Zion, as those of the same blood as the woman and the Lamb but, more importantly, as those who have followed the Lamb. They are with the Lamb because they had overcome Satan by his redeeming blood and by the word of their testimony (12:11), the word of their testimony being understood here as consisting at least of no lie being found in their mouths (v.5).

Yet the eternal gospel that those of Israel believe is also proclaimed worldwide to "every nation, tribe, language and people" (v.6). A not-too-late call to believe "the eternal gospel" comes from an angel flying in mid-air.

Everyone is to know Babylon the Great's doom is sealed. And over against hearing of "the eternal gospel" there is the solemn warning to avoid worshipping the beast, for eternal torment awaits those who worship him. The only rest promised is that promised to the dead who "die in the Lord."

Salvation, judgment "have come"

12.13 The 144,000 offspring of the woman with the 12-starred crown stand on Mount Zion as pure ones, followers of the Lamb, first fruits to God and the Lamb, *no lie having been found on their lips* as befitting "the word of their testimony" (12:11).

The hour of judgment has come. Proleptically the coming of the salvation and the power and the kingdom of God has arrived, together with the authority of Christ. Patient endurance is called for on the part of the saints *who obey God's commandments and remain faithful to Jesus* ("who hold to the testimony of Jesus", in other words).

14.K THE TEMPLE (14:14-20)

The heavenly temple of God is considered again (cf.11:19). The prophet had left us contemplating the threat coming from the temple in terms of "flashes of lightning, rumbling, peals of thunder, an earthquake and a great hailstorm" (11:19).

When it says that "the time to reap has come," does it speak of a harvest of the good or the bad? It appears to make sense that on the heels of believers and unbelievers being distinguished from one another—unbelievers will never know rest while believers shall always do so (14:6-13) —that two different harvests are here in mind. The first has to do with reaping the "ripe" righteous, the second with the reaping of the unbelieving. Jesus used to speak of the righteous being harvested at the end of time. What was symbolized by the Ark of the Covenant was to come true: the righteous would be saved, the unrighteous meeting with the wrath of God who is to appear majestic to all (11:19 once more).

The second harvest is threatening: An angel, "who had charge of the fire," calls on the Son of Man to put forth his sickle and execute a rather localized judgment—that issues in the trampling of the grapes of wrath outside the city of Jerusalem. The prophets of old foretold the gathering of the world's nations against Jerusalem.

The temple

12.14 An angel comes out of God's heavenly *temple*. *The time has come* to reap, as *the harvest of the earth* is ripe—first, that of the ripeness of the righteous being implied.

On the other hand, there has been a ripening unto fierce judgment. Another angel comes from God's heavenly *temple* to execute it.

The *great city* of Jerusalem, where the bodies of the two witnesses lay in the street after the Beast slays them, where the Lord was crucified (11.8), is the place around where the grapes of divine wrath are trampled on.

14.J COMPLETION (15:1-8)

With the seven plagues, God's wrath on earth will be completed.

We have been prepared to understand more fully "the who and where" of the time of the seven bowls being poured out. We know about the Beast, who the saints are, where the last great battle will be pitched—Revelation 11 to 14 gives us insight into such things.

Yet, here we learn that once God's wrath is completed, not only will those who were victorious over the beast rejoice and sing, but all the nations will come and worship before God. We are to understand by "nations" it is meant that among the nations it is the survivors of the seven plagues who will worship.

John fully discovers that what was to follow in the blowing of the seventh trumpet and the outpouring of the bowls of God's wrath was indeed sweet as honey to the mouth but bitter to the stomach (10:10) —the sweetness lying in the saints being victorious over the Beast and singing of victory (vv.2,3), sweetness lying in all nations coming to worship God (v.4), and the bitterness through contemplating the destruction of many of the world's peoples when the plagues are poured out in divine anger.

The angel astride the sea and the land had sworn "by him who lives forever and ever" (10:6), as he swore concerning the certainty of God's full wrath, having in mind the blowing of the seventh trumpet. The seventh trumpet gives way to the seven angels with the bowls of "the wrath of God, who lives forever and ever" (v.7).

Completion

12.15 The mystery of God will be accomplished (10:7), and God's wrath is then *completed*. Coming down through the outpouring of the seven bowls is the wrath of God, *who lives forever and ever.*

14.1 SEVEN INTENSE JUDGMENTS (16:1-18:24)

The seven bowls of God's wrath follow on from the blowing of the seven trumpets, both judgments more severe than those under the seals. Then, of the trumpets and the bowls, the outcome to do with the bowls is the severest. As the world's peoples refuse to repent, so the judgments increase in their intensity.

The passage to do with the bowls is of some length—not only because the bowls are the final expression of divine anger, but because of the complications to do with the rise and ascendancy of the Beast in the presence of a figure previously unmentioned under the seals and trumpets in the Apocalypse. Strange is the figure of the Woman of the Beast, who carries the title Babylon the Great. Much attention is devoted by John to the fall of the Woman, whose capitalistic and pleasure-loving ways had captivated the world until the seemingly sterner and enforcing power of the Beast conquered her and in her stead began to enchant the world.

The effects of the seven trumpets and the seven bowls mirror one another in a remarkable way, even though the bowls will unleash greater terror—

FIRST TRUMPET	FIRST BOWL
Hail and fire and blood,	The breaking out of
With much burning	painful and ugly sores
SECOND TRUMPET	SECOND BOWL
Sea turning into blood,	Sea turning into blood,
Death in the sea	Death in the sea

THIRD TRUMPET	THIRD BOWL
Death in rivers and springs Of blood	Death in rivers and springs of blood

FOURTH TRUMPET	FOURTH BOWL
Heavenly bodies plunge the world in darkness	The sun scorches with fire

FIFTH TRUMPET	FIFTH BOWL
Torture preventing death and causing "agony"	In darkness the painful and ugly sores cause "agony"

SIXTH TRUMPET	SIXTH BOWL
Four angels released at "the Euphrates" to slay tortuously	Is poured out on "the Euphrates," and the nations are demonically drawn to battle at Armageddon

SEVENTH TRUMPET	SEVENTH BOWL
The world's kingdom becomes the kingdom of the Lord and his Christ	The cities of the nations collapse

Poised between the fourth trumpet and the fifth (8:13), John beheld an angel flying in mid-air and crying out "Woe! Woe! Woe!" The three angels to follow with trumpets—the fifth and the sixth and the seventh—will rain down judgments with great and dire effect. The third woe is to be the severest of all, as it has to do with ushering in the outpouring of the seven bowls (11:14). Mirroring uniquely the earlier three words of woe (8:13) are the woes pronounced on Babylon as she falls. Three times it is proclaimed: "Woe! Woe! O great city . . . " (18:10, 16, 19). The three cries of woe are unique to the episodes that mirror each other in Revelation.

Seven intense judgments

12.16 *Seven angels* pour out the bowls of wrath. *The sea turns to blood, rivers and springs turn to blood, the sun* scorches people with fire, men gnaw their tongues in *agony* as they bear in darkness their ugly and painful sores. Still, *they refuse to repent,* with a refusal reflecting that which occurs after the woe of the sixth trumpet (9:20f.)

The sixth angel pours out his bowl on *the Euphrates.* "Woe! Woe, O great city . . . " is the cry that goes up on the fall of Babylon.

14.H SALVATION OF GOD (19:1-10)

At the fall of Babylon there is much rejoicing by a great heavenly multitude. They sing of salvation belonging to God. So too do the 24 elders and the four living creatures. A voice from the throne exhorts God's servants to praise him. Then the great multitude no longer praise the fall of Babylon but the rise of God's Kingdom, as well as the long-anticipated "supper of the Lamp." The term "a great multitude" is only in the passages that mirror one another in more than one way. In Revelation 7 "a great multitude" also sing of salvation belonging to God, and exclaim "Amen!" And in a similar vein to Revelation 7 the 24 elders and the four living creatures sing and resound with their "Amen."

Like Revelation 7 the saints are described as God's servants and who, in their service, are also satisfied of their hunger and have their thirst slaked forever. In Revelation 19 they are seen as having the joy of feasting at the marriage supper of the Lamb . In 7 the Lamb is depicted as their shepherd who feeds them, while in 19 he is seen as the Lamb to marry his bride the New Jerusalem and who invites the saints to what will be a wedding feast.

Salvation of God

12:17 *A great multitude* in heaven is seen wearing *fine linen* (compare this with the white robes of 7:9), and crying out loudly that *"salvation belongs to God." The 24 elders and the four living creatures fall down and answer with "Amen."* The victorious saints *serve God.* They are invited to *the wedding supper of the Lamb,* and are therefore blessed.

14.G WHITE HORSE, WHITE CLOTHING, WORLD RULERS (19:11-21)

There appears before John a white horse and a Rider. This time Christ is viewed not as the Lamb (see 6:16) but as a warrior-king. Psalm 45 may have

14 Mirrors in Revelation

sprung to the seer's mind, as that song combines the concept of the God-Man with that of a warrior-king, who in conquest will marry.

While some scholars dismiss the coming of the Rider on the white horse as a personal appearance, everything here points to the long-anticipated personal advent of Christ himself. It would be strange if this scene did not stand for his personal Return, as no other passage in this book of prophecy describes it, in a book that prophetically anticipates it and views it as the climax of history.

God's servants become fellow-warriors with him who is appropriately called at this point "the Word of God," as he will carry out God's word and bring to an end the confederation of evil on the earth and install God's Kingdom. The Beast is accompanied by "the Kings of the earth," along with their armies to meet the Word of God in battle.

The lesser rider of a white horse (6:1) had done his part to disturb a world ever lolling in false security, so that under the seals, when those more general signs work towards the culmination of the wrath of God being sensed universally, "the kings of the earth" are among men who secretly fear the Final Day (cf.19:19 with 6:15).

White horse, white clothing, world rulers

12.18 Christ appears on a *white horse* as the ultimate conqueror. His fellow-warriors wear fine linen, *white and clean*. God's great supper is that of the world's flesh being devoured by carrion birds, so distinguishing it from the Lamb's wedding supper.

The kings of the earth join the Beast to fight the Word of God.

14.F REIGNING ON EARTH (20:1-15)

At the overthrow of the Beast and the False Prophet, Satan is bound for a thousand years. It is only the Beast and the False Prophet who are thrown in "the fiery lake of burning sulphur" when Christ appears and overthrows the confederation of evil on earth. Satan is merely bound for a time, with him yet to meet his final doom. The martyrs, who had suffered death at the hands of the Beast in their defiance of him, in particular come to life and reign with Christ during the thousand years while Satan is bound.

This mirrors the episode that finds the 24 elders and the four living creatures earlier on prophetically singing a new song about the Lamb purchasing a people for God by his blood so that they may reign as kings and priests on earth (Revelation 5). The 24 elders and the four living creatures were then singing a new song in anticipation of Christ finally returning to earth and enabling God's people to reign at last on the planet.

The kings of the earth join the Beast to fight the Word of God.

Reigning on earth

12.19 With Satan bound and, after many among the nations are struck down with the sword (19:15), and Christ rules the rest with "an iron scepter" (19:15 again), all believers—with the martyrs of the Beast's reign given special attention drawn to them—will be free to *reign with Christ for a thousand years as priests of God and of Christ,* reigning in a way peculiar to the 1000 years, until Satan is released for a short time, and until the unbelieving dead are all judged.

14.E THE DWELLING OF GOD (21:1-4)

God is now seen as dwelling with men—living with them in the renewed (made new again) heaven and earth. In the mirroring passage to 21:1-4—that is 4:1-11—John is called on to "Come up here." There he goes *up* to see God on his heavenly throne, with all the glory and power surrounding it. At the appearance of the new heaven and new earth, the Holy City, the New Jerusalem, which had been prepared for Christ as his bride, *comes down out of heaven from God,* he himself comes down as well to live with men.

It may seem strange to modern ears to contemplate Christ being married to a city. George Peters, the 19th century author of the voluminous *The Theocratic Kingdom,* conceded that to modern ears such a thing seems cold but claimed in ancient times it was not uncommon for royal figures to be viewed as married to the land they loved and prized as their realm. Contrary to popular opinion that the bride of Christ is the church in Revelation, a careful reading requires one to concede that Christ's bride is the New Jerusalem (19:6–9).

Isaiah 62:4 reveals the land of Israel will be called "Beulah", meaning married. "(Beulah) tells of God's tender affection and marital delight in his city."[10]

---

10. McDonald, *Believer's Bible Commentary*

The dwelling of God

12.20 While John ascended in the Spirit to behold the glory of God in heaven, the New Jerusalem will *descend* from heaven to earth, with God dwelling with men so as to live with them!

14.D OVERCOMING (21:5-22:6)

Many of the promises made to the seven churches of Asia will find their fulfilment once the New Jerusalem descends. Each church was exhorted to "overcome," as it is "He who overcomes will inherit all that comes with the renewed heaven and earth" (v.7).

Some churches were threatened with the removal of their lampstands, but all of them received promises that if they overcame as individuals, then the things enumerated in this passage will everlastingly be theirs.

Overcoming

12.21 "He who *overcomes* will inherit all (that the new heaven and new earth shall bring about)." *The second death* will not hurt any overcomer, for its place of a fiery lake of burning sulphur will be for the unbelieving ... The New Jerusalem (3:13) is *the Holy City*. The promise of being a pillar in God's temple (3:12) means being a pillar in God and the Lamb, as they are the temple (v.22). *The nations* over whom Christ will give us authority as overcomers (2:26) will comprise those who will walk by the light of the glory of God.

Then there are the promises of having one's name in *the Lamb's book of life*, of tasting *the tree of life*.

14.C FALLING DOWN TO WORSHIP (22:7-11)

Jesus promises to come soon (v.7). Having seen things pertaining to the future, John fell down at the feet of the angel who showed these things to him, before him who aided him in seeing them. The angel seemed vested with so great a power that John was overwhelmed by it, and fell to worship.

He was chided in doing so. The angel bade him to worship God. This enlightens us as to the person of Jesus, before whose feet John also fell, only he earlier fell at Jesus' feet "as though dead." For the person of Jesus was more awesome than that of the angel. Moreover, we observe John was not chided for falling at Jesus' feet. It may not have been strictly worship on John's part—more fear than anything—but he was not chided for falling at Jesus' feet. In a sense he had a right to fear, but then he was told not to fear.

Revelation begins with Jesus telling John to write down "what you have seen, what is now and what will take place later." Towards the end, when all has been seen, the angel tells John, "Do not seal up the words of the prophecy of this book."

Falling down to worship

12.22 Jesus says there is blessing for those who keep the words of the prophecy in the book—the words Jesus told John to write. *The words are not to be sealed up.*

14.B ALPHA AND OMEGA (22:12-17)

Once more Jesus says, "I am coming soon." This time he spells out what is meant by the blessedness he promises (v.7). The blessedness has to do with the reward he has in reserve according to what has been done.

Jesus assumes the attribute ascribed to the Lord God at the beginning of the book. No less is he "the Alpha and Omega, the First and the Last, the Beginning and the End." On the contemplation of Revelation, no-one ought to be surprised to learn Jesus is equal to God the Father, even though at times he himself appears to allude to his manhood by calling God "My God."

As the Alpha and the Omega, he has power to bestow blessing on all those who wash their robes, authority to bless them with the right to the tree of life and enter the gates of the city of the New Jerusalem.

Strictly speaking, John was originally given the testimony of Jesus for the sake of the seven churches by the angel John falsely worshipped , but the testimony was for all churches of all ages, all saints of every generation, doubtlessly of particular inspiration for those living in the End Times and who are to be exhorted to persevere in the midst of the great tribulation to come (13:10,18; 14:13).

That Jesus is to be "the ruler of the kings of the earth" (8:5) means he shall carry out the ancient promises concerning the Davidic kingdom, hence Jesus calls himself "the Root and the Offspring of David" (v.16). He was before David so he was the Root of David, yet he came after David so that he was David's Offspring!

Jesus says "I am coming soon!" while the Spirit and the bride say "Come!" Readers and listeners of the book of Revelation are beckoned to come if they thirst for what Jesus offers before Jesus himself comes to set up his Davidic Kingdom. In the light of the prospect of being in the New Jerusalem and not forever cast away, the Spirit with considerable persuasion calls people to slake their thirst with "the free gift of the water of life."

A full description of what it means for God and his Son to be "the Alpha and the Omega, the First and the Last, the Beginning and the End" appropriately appears at the beginning and the end of the whole prophecy, appearing in the passage of 1:4-8 and here.

Alpha and Omega

12.23 Jesus identifies himself with the Almighty (1:8) by *declaring "I am the Alpha and the Omega, the First and the Last, the Beginning and the End."* His testimony is relayed by an angel to John for the churches. Jesus is *the Root and the Offspring of David,* which qualifies him to be the world's ruler according to the ancient promises.

14.A THE TESTIMONY (22:18-20)

The prophecy began with a promise of a blessing to those who read aloud or listen to its words. As a counterbalance, a warning rings out here at the end for anyone who contemplates adding to or taking away any words of the book.

Jesus then adds to the testimony of John, who testified to everything he saw—"that is, the word of God and the testimony of Jesus Christ" (1:2). As we come to the end of the grand chiasmus of Revelation, our attention is drawn one final time to the way there is much in Revelation that is mirrored on either side of that passage concerning the rise of the Beast in the center of the book. Our attention needs to be drawn yet again to the grand mirroring in the entire prophecy, our understanding of Revelation being broadened considerably through amplification, a counterbalancing of concepts, through explication of various doctrines, through both comparisons and contrasts.

Whether John the seer was conscious of the chiastic structure of the prophecy or not, his book does fall out in the order of a chiasmus, helping us to reap more than we anticipated when reading it as a "straight" work. Of course, much is gained without being aware of the chiastic structure, but more profit comes our way by delving deeper through the chiasmus.

To return to the end of Revelation and concerning the testimony: John had a testimony, a testimony about Jesus and a testimony that came from Jesus himself. And Jesus himself says at the very end He testifies to all John wrote. And by endorsing John's testimony, he says yet again, "I am coming soon" (see vv.7, 13, as well as v.20).

After witnessing all he saw, John can only say gladly, "Amen. Come Lord Jesus."

The book ends with the prayerful wish of the much-needed grace for God's people.

The testimony

12.24 John *warns* against adding to or taking away from the book of Revelation. Both the threat of the plagues described in the book and the deprivation of not sharing in the new heaven and new earth lends solemnity to the warning.

Jesus himself endorses or *testifies* to John's words, his Return alluding to the judgment yet to come, as well as revealing his coming will *soon* bring salvation to his people, causing John to sigh for him to return.

The end.

www.ingramcontent.com/pod-product-compliance
Lightning Source LLC
Chambersburg PA
CBHW062002180426
43198CB00036B/2145